Ready to start your own business?

BELINDA STEFFAN

Ready to start your own business?

Prepare to think and act like a successful entrepreneur

PEARSON
Prentice Hall
BUSINESS

Harlow, England • London • New York • Boston • San Francisco • Toronto • Sydney • Singapore • Hong Kong
Tokyo • Seoul • Taipei • New Delhi • Cape Town • Madrid • Mexico City • Amsterdam • Munich • Paris • Milan

PEARSON EDUCATION LIMITED

Edinburgh Gate
Harlow CM20 2JE
Tel: +44 (0)1279 623623
Fax: +44 (0)1279 431059
Website: www.pearsoned.co.uk

First published in Great Britain in 2008

ISBN: 978-0-273-71510-8

British Library Cataloguing-in-Publication Data
A catalogue record for this book is available from the British Library

Library of Congress Cataloging-in-Publication Data
Steffan, Belinda.
    Ready to start your own business? : prepare to think and act like a successful entrepreneur.
        p. cm.
    Includes bibliographical references.
    1. New business enterprises. 2. Entrepreneurship. I. Title
    HD62.5.S7414 2008
    658.1'1--dc22

                                                                    2007050118

10 9 8 7 6 5 4 3 2 1
12 11 10 09 08

Typeset in 10.5/14.5pt IowanOldSt BT by 3
Printed and bound in Great Britain by Henry Ling Ltd, Dorchester, Dorset

The Publisher's policy is to use paper manufactured from sustainable forests.

Contents

Acknowledgements

I set out to write this book to help entrepreneurs learn some of the basics of setting up and operating a business prior to actually doing so. During my years of experience as a management accountant and consultant within both large and small businesses, I have been constantly amazed by how little preparation goes into business planning prior to the actual launch of a business. Much money is lost and many mistakes are made and I often hear the words, 'If only we had known that before . . .'

This book is drawn from the sum of my professional experiences over the past 12 years – the good and the bad. I therefore thank everyone I have ever worked with as this book is a culmination of a million little business experiences, not to mention quite a few big ones. Working with the great – and the not so great – has taught me that the keys to success in business are to keep on learning and to keep an open mind.

Introduction

Many people dream about starting their own business, to realise their ambition to be an entrepreneur, or to give themselves and their families a better life. This is an admirable dream and it has inspired many people. However, dreaming about leaving the day job behind and setting up on your own is one thing; actually doing it and becoming a successful entrepreneur is another one entirely.

The chances of success when running a small business enterprise are greatly increased if you plan, prepare, research, think and develop as much as you can before you actually open for business. While this time of planning can be frustrating for those who just want to get on with starting the business, it is crucial to learn valuable lessons before you face your customers.

Ready to start your own business? is aimed at people who have a good business idea as well as ambition. While your level of business experience is of course important, operating your own company is vastly different from being an employee, so even if you have many years of experience, you will need to go back to basics when starting up on your own.

The content of this book is the result of many years of working with small businesses and seeing how things should be done, not to mention how things can go terribly wrong without good planning and the ability to ask for help. *Ready to start your own business?* is a summary of twelve years of day-to-day, practical experience with directors, shareholders, senior management, operational and junior level staff. It brings together their opinions and experience to provide the reader with practical guidance.

The sections in this book cover the main aspects of starting up and operating a small business. Work through the sections and the activities and really give thought to the thorough planning of your concept so you will be as prepared as possible for the real thing.

Good luck.

Belinda Steffan
ACMA, MSc (SMA)

About You

You are the foundation of your business. The process of starting your own business starts here – with you. This section will help you understand what has brought you to this point and why you are reading this book. Ask yourself, 'Why do you want to set up a business?'

Chapter 1 – Do you have what it takes?

Your starting point is what you know, what you want to develop, how you plan and ultimately, how you put every piece of the puzzle together to produce a productive, profitable company. Achieving this is no easy feat, though the risk of setting up a new business is dramatically reduced if you understand yourself before jumping into a new business venture with both feet.

Chapter 2 – What are your objectives?

Objectives are important as they provide clarity of purpose. They are also the foundation of the business plan, so delve into what you really want from this business in terms of personal and business objectives.

Chapter 3 – What are your strengths and weaknesses?

Understanding your strengths and weaknesses is important as they are the cornerstone of your business potential. Reviewing them will flag where you need to develop and improve and even whether or not you're ready for this journey.

Chapter 4 – How do you make the transition to become an entrepreneur?

Finally, we'll look at the transition from your old (or current) job to being your own boss. So many people yearn for the opportunity to be their own boss, without truly understanding the impact it will have on every part of their lives. Find out how to make the change as smooth as possible and avoid some common pitfalls.

1

Do you have what it takes?

Do you consider yourself an entrepreneur already or are you hoping to learn the required skills along the way? This chapter will answer questions about your starting point and your personal journey to becoming an entrepreneur. When you ask yourself, 'Do I have what it takes?' you are asking yourself whether you have the skills, determination, good fortune and confidence necessary to become a successful entrepreneur. Do you have the ability to build a successful business that can meet your objectives, based on a Big Idea that you have developed? There is a lot to think about before you will be able to answer these questions. The main question at this stage is – are you strong enough personally to become the foundation stone for your business?

The term 'entrepreneur' is used a lot these days, but what exactly does it mean? An entrepreneur is defined as a 'risk-taking person, somebody who sets up and finances new enterprises to make a profit'. In the context of this book, an entrepreneur is not about becoming a tycoon, an industrialist or a business mogul; instead we are focusing on an individual with a commercially viable Big Idea, a unique set of skills and a lot of determination who will achieve success by creating a successful business enterprise through a combination of factors.

The first question to ask yourself is, 'Am I a risk taker?' If you answer no to this question, then the odds are that you are not an entrepreneur – yet. If you answer yes, then you have the first and most important trait of a true entrepreneur. An entrepreneur must remember, value and understand the basic foundations of good business practice. Factors such as emotions, ego, misinformation and outside influence can get the better of all of us on occasion. When you can sense this happening, focus on your basic business priorities to help you regain your clarity. It works – every time!

There are some personal and academic attributes that every entrepreneur should possess. They are crucial to success. It is not just about making numbers add up; an entrepreneur must be able to thrive as an individual, a team member, a leader, an administrator, a mentor and a student. Some techniques can be learned from a course or book; other characteristics must be engrained within our personality.

Activity: Have you got what it takes to be an entrepreneur?

Try this questionnaire and see how you rate as a potential entrepreneur. Rate yourself on a scale of 0 to 4 (0 = very strongly disagree, 4 = very strongly agree). Refer your total to the results below.

No.	Statement	0	1	2	3	4
1	I am comfortable with taking risks.					✓
2	I am organised and methodical.			✓		
3	I feel that I have enough time available to dedicate to my next project.					✓
4	I feel that I have sufficient financial support to allow for potential earning downtime.				✓	
5	I am self-motivated.					✓
6	I believe in my Big Idea.					✓
7	I am confident in front of both small and large groups.					✓
8	I can take constructive criticism well.				✓	
9	I am good at selling.				✓	
10	I bring out the best in other people.				✓	
	TOTALS					

Calculate the points scored in each statement and add them together to gain a total for the 10 questions. The scale below will tell you which category you belong to. Bear in mind this is your starting point. While these traits can be learned or developed over time, you do need to have an awareness of what is required of you personally from very early on in your career as an entrepreneur.

Points Scored	What does it mean?
30–40	You have a true entrepreneurial spirit and the key characteristics that are essential to become a successful entrepreneur. Remain aware of the need for these attributes and continue to build upon these throughout your career.
20–29	While you have many attributes that are congruent with an entrepreneurial career, you should continue to learn about what is involved in this type of business discipline.
10–19	You have some key characteristics of a successful entrepreneur, though you also need to work on certain areas. Study the full list and identify your areas of weakness. These are the areas that need your immediate attention and should be developed. However your whole skill set should be kept up to date.
0–9	You appear to have some way to go in order to develop your skills into those of an entrepreneur. It is important to recognise what may be lacking from your skill set or personal make-up. It is best to recognise and acknowledge these areas so that improvements can be made at an early stage.

I recommend that people take this test when they start out and then do it again once they are 12 months into their entrepreneurial journey. The results are usually very interesting. Very rarely are both sets of answers remotely alike!

The questionnaire is designed to give you an idea of some of the personal characteristics that are important to a budding entrepreneur. These don't change. You'll need an awareness of these attributes from day one and you'll still need them when you're sitting on investments worth over £10 million. Let's look at each of the questions to examine why they are so important. We'll also be covering each point many times throughout the book as they, along with good business practice, are the cornerstones of being a success in business.

How do you approach risk?

Do you think you are risk averse? How do you know? Taking a risk means that when you approach a particular situation you are happy to gamble on the outcome. The chances that entrepreneurs take are always calculated risks; there will always remain a large element of jeopardy. However, the threat of loss of resources has to be weighed up against the potential gain.

How organised and methodical are you?

It is absolutely essential to be able to simultaneously manage yourself, a project, and perhaps a team of internal and external individuals who are critical to the success of your project. Organisation and following a strict methodological path are key characteristics of success. You need the ability to think logically, set down a plan and carry it out in an efficient and effective manner.

How much time do you have available to dedicate to your project?

Time is money. An old adage and one that remains very true today, especially in a modern, competitive business environment. You will soon discover that time is one of your most precious resources and you will never have enough to do everything you need to do. Prioritisation is crucial when it comes to planning your schedule.

Can you allow for potential earnings downtime?

Financial constraints are often the key limitation to great ideas becoming financially viable in business. While setting up your project, you may decide to leave your full-time role entirely or merely cut back on your hours. There will come a time, however, when you will need to spend business hours developing your project, which may not generate sufficient revenue to pay a salary. If this is necessary, it is essential that you have sufficient financial contingency for earnings downtime. Your time and that of the people you hire to perform tasks for your project will weigh heavily on your financial resources.

How self-motivated are you?

What placed you on the road to becoming an entrepreneur? If it was all your own doing, then self-motivation shouldn't be an issue. However, if you needed a bit of a push to get the ball rolling, you need to assess the reasons why. Poor self-esteem, lack of confidence, fear, or sheer laziness are not included on the list of key characteristics of an entrepreneur!

How much do you believe in your Big Idea?

More than anyone else on the planet, you need to believe in your Big Idea. You will need to show unbridled enthusiasm to a number of different parties and this can't waiver at any point. Whatever you need to do to retain enthusiasm in your project, do it.

How confident are you?

To be a successful entrepreneur you will need to have confidence in yourself, your idea, your business plan and subsequent adaptations of it. Having the confidence to operate within both small and large groups is an essential component of being successful in business. The scope of your presentations may extend from a one-to-one meeting with, for example, a potential investor, to the opportunity to speak in front of a large crowd to aid networking – always something you should agree to.

How well can you take constructive criticism?

'This is rubbish!' This is a comment I received from a potential investor when I submitted a business plan for what I thought was a great new venture. Not exactly constructive, but you will hear some things that may be difficult to take and may be upsetting. You can't afford to be disconcerted by such comments; instead find out the reason for the criticism and learn from it.

Do you see yourself as a salesman?

We all have sales ability and whether or not we enjoy 'sales', we all have to 'sell', especially in a business start-up situation. You will need to sell your idea to investors, the bank, stakeholders such as creditors, customers, employees and certainly to your partner – business or otherwise. One can hide away and avoid selling in a large organisation, but in the entrepreneurial world you will always be in sales mode.

Do you bring out the best in other people?

Your role as an entrepreneur and the route to gaining your ultimate goal will be much smoother if you develop positive relationships that provide assistance along the way. By bringing out the best in others, you will build a network of willing individuals who will help you achieve your goals.

Keep learning

Once you have read and understood this book, your answers to the statements on page 6 may change. The whole experience of embarking on an entrepreneurial adventure is about learning some-thing new every day. Keep your eyes and ears open for any piece of new information that will help you hone your craft to become more efficient and knowledgeable.

Conclusion

All of this information is intended to give you a reality check from the start. There is more to starting your own business than having a good idea, being clever or having contacts. You need all of these and more to achieve real success. Once you are confident that you have what it takes to become an entrepreneur, the planning and hard work start, and you are one step closer to achieving your dream.

The key characteristics covered in this chapter are a useful reminder for future use, especially when you feel that you are losing focus. It is easy to lose your way when embarking on a new project, which is why you must constantly step back and look at where you started and where you hope to end up. It's the best way to see if you are off course. Having objectives is a great method for keeping your activities on track, as we will discover in the next chapter.

2

What are your objectives?

Creating a business from your own Big Idea can be an intensely personal endeavour, so it helps to be clear on your personal and business objectives at this point of the process. Later, in sections two and three, we will look at how to develop your Big Idea, and then, in section four, how to transform it into a business plan.

Personal objectives

Why do you want to be an entrepreneur? It's worth giving this a bit of thought to ascertain your personal motivation for entering into this process. Is your motive purely to make a lot of money? Or is it more about work/life balance or creating something to be proud of? Whatever your personal motives, be sure that you have them clear in your mind before proceeding with the business objectives. Personal objectives can impact on business objectives so I always recommend that a key individual in a company should complete this exercise.

Business objectives

I find it helpful, when looking at the overall state of a business, to do it in terms of financial statements. I'll go into this in more detail in section four on planning; in the meantime, I'll adopt the concept of using this structure to show what I mean.

Use the headings from your financial statements and think about what they mean and how they impact on your business. Focusing on each segment of your business at a time will help to focus the mind and ensure you have considered all of your business areas.

Profit and Loss

Revenue – What are your sales objectives? What are you going to sell and how?

Cost of sales – What resources do you need to buy in to make your product, or offer your full and complete service? Who do you want your suppliers to be and why?

Staffing – Who do you want working for you and with you at the set-up stage of your business?

Premises – From where do you want to operate your company and how do you want to be perceived by external parties such as clients, associates or prospective employees?

Overheads – Do you have any other specific objectives for your business, such as providing marketing, PR or other professional services to support the service you are offering?

Balance Sheet

Assets – What are your objectives in terms of your asset base? What physical items do you think you'll need to buy to set up and operate the company?

Liabilities – What are your cash objectives? Will you need to take out immediate borrowings to make the cost of sale or overhead purchases?

Equity – Do you expect to retain a full shareholding in the company or will you split the equity with another investor, director or employee?

Other

Growth – What are your growth objectives? How fast do you expect to grow and how?

Timeframe – How long do you plan to be in this business? Do you plan to sell after a certain period?

These are just some of the questions that you need to ask yourself about your objectives before creating a business plan to sell your Big Idea. You can see that using a structure helps the planning. These business objectives will become the foundation of your business plan. This type of structured thought encourages you to consider the whole of the business when looking at your objectives rather than just profits for example.

Quantifying objectives

The next step is to quantify your objectives by providing a monetary value and possibly a timeframe for each objective. You will need to start by setting both your personal and business objectives as discussed above. Next, you will need to gather as much information as possible to set specific, quantified objectives. This exercise must be carried out before the business plan is created, and I have found it a useful activity for highlighting areas of potential weakness at this early stage where problems can be remedied. The following example shows the importance of quantifying financial security.

When one of my clients first set up his company his objective was to run it as a lifestyle business that would provide him with a good salary while offering his much sought-after work/life balance. He quantified this objective by looking at his basic expenditure and added an amount for savings, which would enable the lifestyle to which he aspired. He came up with the target sum of £75,000 'left over' per year – to use his words. He then calculated roughly how many units of his Big Idea he would have to sell to generate this figure of £75,000, after estimated expenses. After carrying out this activity, he was surprised to find that the number of units he would be required to sell was more than twice what he had originally estimated.

You can see from this example that his objective was not realistic and either the objective or the rough plan would have to change. We'll look at this in more detail in section four on business planning. The characteristics of objectives are:

▶ Realistic

▶ Aggressive

▶ Consistent

▶ Specific

▶ Clear

Your objectives should be realistic, while also being aggressive. A happy balance between the two should be found. For example, to say that your chain of cafes will be bigger than Starbucks in two years, would be unrealistic; but if your objective is to build only two cafes in the first five years, your plan may be seen as lacking ambition and may not attract investment.

The key is to consider your objectives and how others will view them. If you are seeking investment, make your objectives appealing to your audience. If you are not seeking approval from a third party, perhaps planning for only two cafes will meet your objectives.

Objectives must also be consistent. Any incongruity between objectives will create conflict either in the planning or operational phase of your business. This situation is best avoided if possible. For example, if your objectives are to be the market leader while providing a niche product, some may wonder how both are achievable as niche products generally capture a much smaller percentage of the market than a wider reaching product.

Finally, ensure your objectives are specific and have clarity. There is no place for ambiguity in setting objectives, even at this early stage of the process. For example, an objective should be to 'sell 1,000 units within four countries' rather than merely 'sales to a range of countries'.

Conclusion

Ensure your objectives are realistic, appropriately aggressive, consistent, specific and have clarity of purpose. Once set, quantify these objectives and you should have a much clearer picture of how to achieve your dream of starting your own business.

Once you are happy that both your personal and business objectives are clearly defined, it's time to focus on your strengths and weaknesses to identify any areas that should be addressed at this stage of the process.

3

What are your strengths and weaknesses?

Before embarking on your business journey, it is important to understand the personal characteristics that make you perform and operate well. Ultimately, it is this information that will provide the framework and foundation for building your business. A small business is just as much about you, you personality and experience as it is about the business itself. As a start-up venture, external parties will assess you just as closely as the profitability or return on investment of the business proposal, so make sure you know yourself inside out. It may sound obvious, but an assessment of your own objectives and abilities is very important at this stage of your business life as it will highlight areas where your natural skills and abilities lie.

A person who thrives in working with a small team, yet lacks confidence in large groups should opt for a business suited to these skills. While every entrepreneur will need to wear every management hat in their organisation at some point, they will also have individual strengths and weaknesses that should be identified and built upon.

Embrace your strengths, improve your weaknesses

It is widely recognised that people are happier when working to their strengths, so recognise what these are and build upon them to ensure you are creating a working environment that will be satisfying. The key is to embrace your strengths and improve on your weaknesses, but before you can do this, you need to identify what your strengths and weaknesses are.

Activity: Identify your strengths and weaknesses

A useful way to identify strengths and weaknesses in practice is to pretend that you are about to go for an interview for the job of setting up and managing your company. You really want this job and have prepared and researched as much as possible. You have been asked to give your main strengths and weaknesses (top five of each.). Write them down on a piece of paper. Practise explaining them to the 'interviewer'. If it helps, use a friend as the 'interviewer', but I find sitting in front of a mirror works even better.

What did you learn about yourself from this exercise? Did you find it more difficult to come up with weaknesses than strengths or the other way around? Most people struggle with weaknesses as they don't want to admit their flaws, though it is the understanding of these that is the key to maximising your full potential.

Your results will show you which characteristics to embrace and develop as the foundations of your company (your strengths) and which areas require more attention and focus (your weaknesses) before setting up your company.

The idea of preparing for an interview will be useful throughout your life as a small business owner as you will attend plenty of meetings where you will need to pitch your small business (and yourself) to banks, suppliers, investors and potential employees. Understand the concept of the exercise and retain it for future use.

If you struggled with this exercise, consider your strengths and weaknesses in the context of the following three categories:

1. Knowledge (learned information appropriate to the business)
2. Transferable skills (appropriate in any business)
3. Personal traits (makes up your character).

Your five strengths and weaknesses should take account of each of these three sections.

Activity: Strengths and weaknesses checklist

The strengths and weaknesses checklist following, covers both technical and personal attributes. It is designed to highlight areas of small business knowledge and the character traits essential for a budding entrepreneur. Take a few minutes to rate your current level of ability for each task on a scale of 0 to 4 (0 = inexperienced, 4 = skilled) and then add up the totals for each column. Refer to the table on page 24 for an assessment of what your total points mean. The outcome will give you an idea of areas that require further focus as well as areas that will capitalise on your most positive qualities.

Business area	Skill	0	1	2	3	4
Personnel	Hire the right employees for your business.					
	Manage your staff to perform to the best of their abilities and in the best interest of your company.					
	Motivate your staff to perform over and above their previous performance or the performance of others.					
	Manage conflict situations between employees or between an employee and the company.					
Sales	Set the right price for your product to ensure that customers buy it, while maximising profit.					
	Buy from suppliers at a price that maximises your profits.					
	Find your ideal customer base.					
	Make the sale – new and existing customers.					
	Communicate and negotiate with your customers.					
	Provide after-sales service.					
	Manage sales staff who are likely to be remunerated on sales targets.					

Business area	Skill	0	1	2	3	4
Marketing	Initiate advertising ideas and promotions.					
	Ensure a solid and up-to-date knowledge of your market and your competitors.					
	Create a marketing plan that feeds from and into the overall budget. Understand its impact on the whole business.					
	Develop marketing strategies around the objectives of the company.					
	Optimise potential from the available distribution network.					
	Ask yourself how well you know the 4 Ps: price, promotion, product and placement.					
Accounting	Understand the basic financial statements: profit and loss, balance sheet and cashflow.					
	Understand and apply bookkeeping basics.					
	Manage debtors and creditors to maximise the potential of your working capital.					
	Create budgets that can deliver on objectives and can provide an operational plan for staff.					
	Calculate the profitability of one unit of sales and understand its impact on the overall business.					
	Understand the key performance indicators of the business. (See chapter 11.)					
	Develop exact knowledge of the working capital required to operate the business and its sources.					
	Identify any potential investment required for the business to start operations and know where to source the finance.					
	Know the tax implications of a small business in the UK.					

Business area	Skill	0	1	2	3	4
Legal	Understand the basics of contract law: offer and acceptance.					
	Understand the circumstances when you need a contract and when a verbal agreement is sufficient.					
Administrative	Plan labour resources to ensure employees are satisfied and company resources are being used to optimum efficiency.					
	Find the right property for your business. Consider place and price of commercial space.					
Your personal skills	Readiness to present any aspect of your business to a small, medium or large group.					
	Ability to write a clear, concise document in appropriate business language.					
	A good level of computer literacy – especially in Word and Excel.					
	Personal management skills: such as working to deadlines.					
	Ability to remain focused on a task (the detail) and the overall objective (the big picture).					
	You work well alone.					
	You are able to manage others who look to you for guidance and motivation.					
	You understand the concept of risk management by mitigating your company's exposure.					
	You will be supported by your family during the business start-up process.					
	You have a high level of self-belief.					
Totals						

Add together the points scored in each column for each of the 40 questions and refer to the table below to determine which of the categories below you belong to. Bear in mind this result is your starting point. Many of these traits can be learned or developed. However, you need to understand your strengths and weaknesses very early on in your career as an entrepreneur and to have an awareness of what is required of you – both personally and professionally.

As you will see from the table below, a score reflecting a high level of weakness requires immediate action. It is suggested that individuals presenting a score of 39 or less should put their entrepreneurial goals on hold until such time as they understand the realities of owning and running a small business.

Points Scored	What does it mean?
120–160	You are very well prepared to set up a small company. Your strengths in the business world should be embraced and built upon to ensure continued consolidation. You are an asset to your business and your foundation to start a small business is strong. Full steam ahead!
80–119	You are predominately strong in business tasks and performance, though you have now identified some areas of weakness. Use your areas of strength to overcome the weaknesses as your business set-up progresses.
40–79	The results have highlighted your weaknesses. These areas should be noted and improved prior to setting up a business. While some weaknesses can be learned on the job, your weaknesses outweigh your strengths and should be addressed as a priority. Don't forget to capitalise on the areas that showed your strengths.
0–39	Your weaknesses have been identified and should be worked on as a priority before you set up your business. You should use this list of questions and work through it until you are familiar with each section as each skill is an integral requirement for owing and running a small business.

Don't lose hope if you scored low in the above activity. The first step is to identify areas of weakness; the next step is to target these areas for improvement.

Activity: Modelling successful behaviour

Modelling successful behaviour can be a useful way to improve business skills. Think about three positive qualities that you think a successful entrepreneur should have, that you don't currently possess. Once you've written these down, consider how you could develop these traits and overcome your weaknesses.

A client of mine thought that all entrepreneurs should come from a business background. She was afraid that she couldn't start her own business as she had no formal training in business or accounting. She set about learning what she could from other sources, such as experienced businessmen, books, newspapers and the Internet. She took every opportunity she could to learn about what made businesses tick. Her knowledge on the subject increased and she now runs meetings with her investors and other business contacts with confidence.

Conclusion

Your strengths and weaknesses are critical to your success or failure. Make sure you identify your strong points and embrace these. Equally, your flaws can make you vulnerable, so manage your exposure to risk by understanding and resolving your weaknesses through improved learning or understanding.

Increased knowledge about yourself will give you more power and clarity to deal with setting up your business. Remember, your skills provide the foundations for your business and you must be strong enough to provide the business with the stability it needs.

4

How do you make the transition to become an entrepreneur?

You have decided that you have what it takes, you have your objectives clear in your mind and you have spent time identifying your strengths and weaknesses; but how do you make the transition from employee to setting up your own business?

Whether you are employed or have left your job to pursue your own business, there will be a period of transition from one to the other. This transition can be daunting for even the most hard-nosed, seasoned businessman. How can you prepare for the adventure ahead once your safety net is taken away and you are without the resources of a more established company?

Understand why you are making the change

Generally, a career change is triggered by a situation that you want to change, such as working long hours, experiencing conflict, stress, poor remuneration, boredom or lack of a challenge. It is important to identify the reason for your decision to change direction to try to avoid its replication in your new venture. Is your objective realistic? Don't forget that new small business owners are likely to work harder and earn less in the short term than their equivalent salary earners. This is not always the case, but it must be a consideration for anyone planning to make the move from being an employee to being an employer.

For example, your objective might be to set up your new company in order to have more freedom to spend time with your family. Before you begin, ask yourself the following questions. How many hours will your new business require? Will your customers be happy with flexible hours or will they expect you to be available when required? Make sure your new business can meet your personal requirements – and those of your family – so that you avoid disappointment as a result of the new venture.

Establish credibility

Your transition from employee to employer will be smoothed once you establish some credibility in the marketplace. Credibility is about being both trustworthy and seen as an expert in your field. You must show that you are worthy of the confidence of others and that your business idea is plausible. Companies who have traded for years have generally built up a trading history with customers, a credit history with suppliers and are perceived to offer job security to the best employees.

The ways in which your business can gain credibility will be covered later in the book. For now we will focus on you and how to build your own profile.

1. List any exceptional trade deals or projects you have worked on in recent years.
2. Describe your work style and why it will contribute to the success of your new company.
3. Describe your ideal work situation and how you will achieve it.
4. What is your personal unique selling point (USP) and why do you think it will attract people to your business?

5. Make sure you know your Big Idea and its market inside out (we'll cover this in sections two and three).

6. Make sure your personal situation will hold up to scrutiny. Consider factors such as education, skills and financial stability.

The output from the above list of personal selling points will provide you with credibility from which to build your business. Once you are prepared to meet your audience (the bank, investors, suppliers, employees, customers and landlord to name a few), it's time to think about some practicalities of the transition.

Old and new – what do they have in common and what can be learned?

It is likely that there will be some overlap between your old job and your new role as a business owner. Perhaps you have remained in the same industry or the business concepts are similar. Will your customers be found in the same market? Will both your old and new roles draw on the same strengths and highlight the same weaknesses or require the same personal and business skills? What have you learned from your old job that you can apply to your new company? Think about the following transitional tools:

1. *Organisational skills* – For example, project planning tools.

2. *Marketing strategy* – How did your old company go about finding and attracting customers?

3. *Personnel management style* – What positives can you take from your old manager if you liked his style, or what lessons can you learn if his style wasn't considered a success.

4. *Accounting policies* – For example, treatment of expenses and invoicing.

5. *Product development* – How long did it take to develop your former product and what market research was carried out?

6. *Supplier pricing* – Understand the cost of sales and methods used to buy raw materials cost effectively.

7. *Labour resources* – How many people did your former company have and were they being used efficiently? (Most employees have an opinion about how this process can be made better, so consider talking to some people in other departments).

This list could go on and on. Identify what worked and what didn't work well at your old job. Learn from the environment from which you have come. If you're still there, take a look around or think back to your old job and try to apply your knowledge and experience to your new venture. It's amazing what information we capture without realising it, so take the time to recall some of this information now. (A note on the above point: ensure that the transitional tools you use do not breach any terms of contract with your old company. For example, be aware of intellectual property rights – see chapter 16.)

Activity: Your monthly tasks

It can be valuable to write down the general monthly tasks that feature as part of your old job. Use this checklist as your new monthly task list and bear in mind your strengths and weaknesses as identified in chapter three. You need to appreciate that you should be able to do all of these tasks on a regular basis in your new job as a business owner. This simple activity can be the eye-opener required to understand the level of transition required as you move from your old job to your new job.

Your management hats

How many hats can you wear at once? The answer in your new role will have to be 'as many as is required'. It is likely you will need all of these hats every day of your new job. At least being a small business manager is never dull! The top six hats to keep handy are:

- ▶ Manager
- ▶ Sales and marketing executive
- ▶ Accountant
- ▶ Lawyer
- ▶ Personnel manager
- ▶ Researcher and planner

Of course, you don't have to do everything yourself. Use your strengths and weaknesses checklist from page 21 and where an obvious skills gap has been identified, fill it using one of three options:

1. *Hire* – An employee can be hired to fill a role for which you do not have the required skill and will not have the time or energy to learn in the time available, such as financial planning.

2. *Partner* – The option to partner can be beneficial to a small business that may not have sufficient capital to hire a dedicated resource. A common example of this is a sales network built on external distributors.

3. *Develop your own skills* – If time and money allow, you can learn a new skill set or develop existing abilities; or turn a weakness into a strength. Marketing skills are a good example of this as the principles are easily learned and should be tailored to your specific business profile.

What will you miss in the transition from old to new?

Think about the aspects of your old job that you will miss. Most of us take for granted the things that a structured, relatively secure environment can provide, and which a small company may not be able to provide initially. These include:

▶ Working with a team.

▶ Social interaction with colleagues.

▶ A secure salary, without worrying about available funds.

▶ Having a support framework, such as Information Technology (IT) and Human Resources (HR).

▶ Working to a clear, unambiguous job description.

▶ Having your tasks and objectives defined for you.

If there's something that's really important to you in your old position that you feel will be lacking from the new position, try to find a way to bridge the gap.

Two years ago Joe left his job at a large bank to set up his own financial consultancy. He was happy with the change in so many ways – remuneration had improved, as had his work/life balance. He sourced his own customers, but then had a free hand to make business decisions. Every aspect of his new business life worked perfectly, except he missed the social interaction of working with a large group of his peers. The beer after work on Fridays, the banter around the office, even the trip to get a sandwich at lunchtime had gone, and he felt alone. He remedied this by having client meetings out of his office where possible and by increasing his business network. His new network of clients and suppliers became his new source of social interaction at work. Obviously, a level of professionalism and discretion must be upheld, but the situation has satisfied Joe's need for interaction with his peers.

The pros and cons of setting up your own business

In this section we have looked at how to establish yourself as the strong foundation upon which your company can be built. Let's have a last look at some 'pros and cons' of setting up your own business to make sure the reality of your situation is clear.

Advantages	Disadvantages
You have the potential to make a lot more money than you did as an employee.	You will have the personal burden of large financial exposure, likely to be secured on an asset such as your house.
You will have flexibility and variety in your tasks on any given day.	You may spend a lot of time performing administrative tasks rather than focusing on your core business.
You will have job security.	You company may not survive and you could find yourself out of a job.
You will be able to work directly with customers.	You will be the front line for any customer complaints.
You can determine your own remuneration.	Your company may not be generating sufficient profits to pay you the expected or required salary.
You can determine your own working hours to suit your needs.	You are likely to work longer hours and may not have as much time for annual leave.

While I have matched every pro with a con in the above chart to raise awareness of the difficulty of the journey ahead, it should be said that setting up and running a successful business can be intensely gratifying. The positive feeling of setting up a company that will support your family and become a legacy for your children cannot be underestimated. Provided you are well prepared, the positives should outweigh the negatives, but remember to remain alert for problems at all times.

Is it worth the risk?

Undoubtedly, everyone setting up their own business will ask themselves at some point in the process whether it is worth the risk. To answer the question, ask yourself the following two questions:

1. What is at risk?
2. What is the reward objective?

Place the answers to these questions on imaginary weighing scales. The two answers should be in balance. If they are not, you should reassess what you are risking or what you are hoping to achieve from the venture. The principle is that if you are willing to take a certain amount of risk, then you should also expect an equal level of reward to be delivered from the situation. The greater the risk, the greater the reward should be. Successful entrepreneurs are a rare breed in that the calculated risk taken is mitigated by as many factors as possible. Good planning means that the risk can be managed. However, there will always be an element of risk involved in an entrepreneurial situation.

To be a successful entrepreneur, you must be able to assess and manage risk. This means having the ability to calculate the level of risk in any given situation. Your ability to deal with risk will depend on whether you are risk averse or whether you welcome risk with open arms. Uncertainty is inherent in an entrepreneurial situation due to the volatile nature of many projects that map unchartered territory.

Conclusion

The transition from old job to starting your own business will never be totally smooth. Try to anticipate what your new role will encompass and you will be better prepared for day one of being your own boss. Think about what skills and information you can take from your old job and use in your new role as business owner. Inevitably, things will pop up that have not been considered; though if you are prepared and have worked to establish personal credibility then you are already a step ahead.

1

Key points to remember

While education and experience are important for an entrepreneur, there are other key personal characteristics that can be learned and developed:

1. Attitude to risk
2. Organisational skills
3. Time planning
4. Financial planning
5. Self-motivation
6. Self-belief and confidence
7. Public speaking skills
8. Ability to take advice
9. Sales skills
10. People management skills

Identify your personal and business objectives. Once identified, try to quantify these objectives as the basis for further business planning. Objectives should be:

▶ Realistic
▶ Aggressive
▶ Consistent
▶ Specific
▶ Clear

Identify your personal attributes; then learn to embrace your strengths and improve your weaknesses. Think of your strengths and weaknesses in the following categories:

▶ Knowledge (learned information appropriate to the business)

▶ Transferable skills (appropriate in any business)

▶ Personal traits (that make up your character)

Understand why you wish to make the change from employee to entrepreneur. Learn from the old job and apply your knowledge to your new career.

Remember to be flexible and organised. Six of the many hats you will have to wear in your new role are:

▶ Manager

▶ Sales and marketing executive

▶ Accountant

▶ Lawyer

▶ Personnel manager

▶ Researcher and planner

Weigh up the risks and rewards involved in setting up your own company and make sure that running a business is the right decision for you.

About Your Big Idea

This section of the book focuses on your Big Idea; ensuring that it makes commercial sense and enabling you to take the crucial steps necessary to transform your Big Idea into a tangible product that is ready for market research. Turning your dream into a reality can be a learning process for a new entrepreneur. The guidelines and activities in this section will guide you through this often difficult and confusing stage of setting up your own business.

Chapter 5 – What is your Big Idea?

Discover how to find a Big Idea if you don't already have one. If you have a Big Idea, make sure you know it inside out and can explain it fully to a wide ranging and diverse group of interested parties.

Chapter 6 – What makes your Big Idea special?

What is the unique selling point (USP) of your Big Idea? This is a term that will come up a lot in your life as an entrepreneur, so make sure you understand what it means in relation to your business offering.

Chapter 7 – How can you turn your Big Idea into a product?

Follow the Big Idea process map (see page 53) to transform your Big Idea into a tangible product ready for the market. This process includes sourcing raw materials, giving the idea a product name and testing the product so that it is in line with your Big Idea concept and also makes sense as a business proposal.

5

What is your Big Idea?

You have a dream. You want to start your own business. For some, the desire to have the business comes before the Big Idea and for others the company is merely a vehicle to realise the potential of a Big Idea they have nurtured. Whichever category you fit into, it is important that you spend some time thinking about and planning your Big Idea before venturing any further down the path to becoming an entrepreneur.

What if you don't have a Big Idea yet?

First, let us consider those who do not have a Big Idea. Not all of us have had a secret desire to do something, such as revolutionise the gardening industry, from a young age, so if you are struggling to come up with a Big Idea, there are some useful questions following that you can ask yourself.

What do you know about?

Most of us tend to think locally; we think about that which we know, which is good practice for coming up with your Big Idea. If you're a lawyer, your business proposal will be more convincing if you base your concept around your area of expertise rather than plumbing, for example; having said that, you may have a great insight into a plumbing revolution, so it's important to keep your mind open.

What experiences have you had?

Consider whether your experiences could become the framework of a business concept. For example, if your work experience has given you a solid foundation in the property market, you may well base your Big Idea around this market as you already have useful and relevant knowledge. Experiences don't have to be work-related; personal or social experiences can be equally as important. Perhaps travelling abroad has shown you a task that is performed better in other countries than in the UK and you could use this different behaviour to create a Big Idea.

What do you want to do?

You are setting up your own business, so it is important that you enjoy what you do so that your interest will provide motivation to get you through the tough days. Base your Big Idea around what you want to do. You will end up having more enthusiasm for the entire project, which will be obvious to important parties such as investors and customers.

Do any products on the market bother you or someone you know?

Have you come across a product that annoys you? Do you think it could be better? Perhaps there is an opportunity to take an existing product and improve it sufficiently so that it becomes a new Big Idea. So many new business ideas emerged out of frustration with the limitations of the current market offering, so look around you and think about what can be improved.

Answering the four questions above will start leading you toward your Big Idea. Note down your ideas and hopefully inspiration will

> **Activity: Find out how people would like their lives improved**
>
> It can be interesting and useful to ask your colleagues (if you are still employed) or friends about their day-to-day activities and experiences within their business and social settings. Ask them if there is anything that really bothers them about life. While sifting through the issues that need remedying you may come up with a seed of an idea that can grow into a Big Idea.

strike. When you have a few conceptual ideas, apply the following four points as a sense check:

1. *Keep it simple* – Your concept should be kept simple at all times. Don't feel the need to overcomplicate a product just to stand out from the crowd. Potential investors and customers have to understand your Big Idea and what you are trying to provide the market.

2. *Familiarity* – Do you already know or, realistically, can you find out enough information about your concept to make it a genuine Big Idea?

3. *Limitations* – While 'blue sky' thinking is great, your Big Idea will need to work in practice, so try to keep your concepts grounded and realistic.

4. *Originality* – Your Big Idea must not already exist in its current form. It's ok to produce an existing product better or cheaper, but your Big Idea must have a certain amount of originality for it to have any chance of success.

From small seed to Big Idea

Once you have your seed concept, it must grow into a fully fledged Big Idea. This means that you should be able to clearly identify detailed components of the concept which, when added together, become your Big Idea. The following chart distinguishes between the seed of an idea and the Big Idea to come from it using everyday products in an office as examples.

Product	Seed	Big Idea
Post-it notes	A better way to remind us of information or to pass notes to another party without them getting lost.	Small squares of note paper that can stick to any surface, be removed and reused many times resulting in no more lost notes.
Tipp-ex	The ability to cover up written or typed mistakes.	A white, quick drying liquid which is applied to erroneous text, which can then be typed on or written over.

The key to this distinction is the ability to define your Big Idea and understand the path taken to bring it about.

How well can you communicate your Big Idea?

You should know everything there is to know about your Big Idea. Every conceivable question should have been asked and discussed until an answer can be given in an instant. It is common to become too close to a project we have worked on for a while, so take a step back and try to think about your Big Idea from an outsider's perspective.

You are a computer engineer and you have an idea that will revolutionise the way computer games are played. Are you looking at your Big Idea objectively or just from the technical perspective? Have you considered whether you will be able to answer questions from areas other than the technological specification, such as customer behaviour or pricing?

It is possible to overuse jargon or buzz-words, thus confusing the layman. Bear in mind that many parties you encounter on your business journey will not have the same education or experience as you, so tone down your language to cater for a wider audience.

Activity: Ask a trusted friend for feedback

Find a friend who has no detailed knowledge of your Big Idea or its market. Give them the following list of questions. Speak to them for five minutes about your Big Idea and ask them to check off each question as you cover it in sufficient detail for them to understand the answer. Do they feel that you have answered all of the questions?

	Question	Answered in sufficient detail to understand	Did not answer in sufficient detail to understand
1	What does the product do?		
2	Why is it better than anything I already buy?		
3	How does the product work?		
4	Why will it help me?		
5	Is it used with other products or on its own?		
6	How will it make my life easier?		
7	Can I afford it?		

Note – this activity is quite generic and the questions relating to your business may be more tailored to your specific market and idea.

Define your Big Idea

You have passed the five minute test; now it is important to further refine your Big Idea. You should be able to define it clearly in one sentence. This can be quite difficult to achieve as most of us tend to use more words than are necessary to paint a picture. Practise being concise.

> **Activity: Practise being concise**
>
> Choose any item around you. In one sentence, describe its purpose and why it is important to the user. Now apply this concept to your Big Idea. It may take a few attempts before you make sure you cover all of the important points and leave out all of the unnecessary words but it is important that you have this clarity of thought about your Big Idea.

We'll expand the detail about your Big Idea in the next chapter when we look at research and marketing. You can expand your clear, concise message once you come to the business planning section of the process (see section four). Regardless of the complexity of your Big Idea, one sentence should be all it takes to ensure you get your message across.

What's your message?

What are you trying to say to your market with your Big Idea? Is your message that this product will perform better than everything else on the market because it works faster? Or is it a completely new, revolutionary idea that will amaze and astound customers? The purpose of your Big Idea should be understood by a layman through your message.

Why is now the time?

Consider why you have chosen this time to start your own business. Make sure that it is the right time, not just for you, but also for your Big Idea. Is the market ready for your idea or has an opportunity to enter a market just been missed? Why is the time right now? The answer to this question will become an important part of your business proposal.

Conclusion

You have your Big Idea and you can describe it in a clear, succinct sentence. Your message to the customer is clear and you know that now is the right time to move forward. It's time to better understand the detail of your Big Idea and ensure that it is sufficiently special to have a chance at launching into the market.

CHAPTER SIX

What makes your Big Idea special?

Start this chapter by keeping your one sentence description of your Big Idea firmly in your mind. It is this description (as covered in the previous chapter) and its message that will be the basis of understanding what makes your Big Idea special.

What's the Big Idea?

Many people have tried and failed to set up new businesses. One of the main reasons for failure is that the market doesn't want or need what they are providing. Bearing this in mind, apply the following reasoning to your Big Idea:

- Has your product been invented yet?
- If it has, are you improving on the existing offering?
- If it hasn't, are you providing what the customer wants or needs?

If the answer is yes to at least one of these questions, then you're heading in the right direction. The next step is to make sure people will want to buy what you're offering.

What is my unique selling point (USP)?

Every Big Idea should have a unique selling point (USP). This is a feature of your product that will make customers stand up and take notice of what you are offering to them. Without a USP, your Big Idea will have no clear competitive advantage and is unlikely to become a great success. It is hard to break into a market and compete with existing products, so make sure you think about what sets your Big Idea apart from the pack.

What is a USP?

The following statements are examples of USPs:

- A new feature in an existing product range
- The ability to perform a task that nothing else can do nearly as well
- The only one of its kind to hit the market

The following are services, not USPs:

- Great customer service
- Friendly staff
- Money back guarantee

Creating a product with a USP is your opportunity to make investors and customers raise their eyebrows and say, 'Really, now that is interesting.' Make sure your Big Idea is unique and special and it should sell.

Your Big Idea must have sufficient differentiation from other products that people will pay for it. Most people don't part with their money easily, so it's important to make sure you can offer the customer something that is unique or better or cheaper than anything else on the market.

Some examples of popular, successful USPs include:

▶ *Mark Warner* – 'Holidays that provide comprehensive childcare, while maintaining the luxury element from a holiday that so many parents miss after having children.'

▶ *M&M chocolates* – 'Melt in your mouth, not in your hand.' A simple, yet effective USP.

▶ *Boots Protect and Perfect Serum* – This product recently sold out in the UK as it was backed up by scientific research reporting that it was more effective than many other high-profile products already on the market.

If your product has a USP it should be able to compete against similar products in the market, not purely on price, but on features too, which ultimately can make your offering more profitable. So start thinking about product differentiators now.

Don't forget that customers must understand your USP or they won't understand why they should buy it, let alone pay a premium for it. Don't get too technical or the whole point will be missed by the very people you are trying to attract – firstly investors, then customers.

Do others share your enthusiasm?

Enthusiasm is essential to an entrepreneur – blind optimism, however, can be a dangerous liability. Now is the time for a reality check to test just how good your Big Idea is perceived to be.

There is a difference between a product being 'good' and a product being so exceptional that people will not only buy it, but will even pay a premium for it. Make sure your Big Idea is as good as you think it is. Sometimes it's easy to get too close to something we work on day in day out, so try to regain some perspective by asking the opinion of others.

Market testing is a proven way to do this. We'll cover this in more detail in section three; however for now, it is worth testing the market to find out if others share your enthusiasm.

Activity: Using market research

Use the following steps to carry out a small sample market analysis on the viability of your Big Idea.

1. Be clear about the features of the product that will be (or has been) developed from your Big Idea.

2. Determine the target market for your Big Idea. You can be quite general at this stage of your market research, though try to identify the sex, age and spending power of your target customer base. For example, the target market (or demographic) may be classified as middle-class men in their 30s.

3. Use a prototype sample if you have one, otherwise a strong, clear definition of the product will be fine. If you are using a prototype, make sure it functions exactly as it should.

4. Choose a small sample population from your chosen demographic (around five will suffice for this activity). They can be friends or colleagues at this stage as you are simply testing whether you are being realistic as to the commercial viability of your Big Idea. The sample should reflect your target customer base as much as possible in terms of demographic, assumed knowledge, experience and attitudes.

5. The sample population should be asked to sit in a room with the prototype or sketch or description of the product for ten minutes. You should not be present initially. Encourage them to discuss the product and write down comments.

6. Enter the room after ten minutes and take questions and respond to feedback.

This is an extremely useful activity to perform at this stage and it could save you a lot of expense and time further down the track. You should take the feedback and use it to develop and improve

---

your Big Idea. Listen to people if they say they wouldn't buy the product or service and ask them why not. You may need to go back to basics to understand why your product may not appeal to others as it does to you.

Will it have sufficient demand in the wider market?

Your small sample population has given you feedback and you're still convinced that your Big Idea is the next big thing. Now think about the wider market. Will there be sufficient demand to support your new company and its cost base? Your product must be able to sell enough units to qualify for becoming the product base of a company.

We will look at this in more detail in the marketing and planning sections of this book (see sections three and four). At this point, sense check how attractive your product will be to the wider market. Is your Big Idea too 'niche' to make the required volume of sales? Do you need to adapt it slightly to make it attractive to a larger customer base? Don't limit your potential by making your product too special or unique. There is a delicate balance between a feature that is a USP and one that is so niche that only five people will be interested in your product.

A twin buggy for same size babies will limit your market only to those parents and carers who have twins. Developing your product to enable one seat to be replaced with a toddler seat widens the market to include those who have a baby and a toddler, which is a much wider audience that the twin market.

Conclusion

Now that you have your Big Idea and you are sure that it's a great idea with a key differentiator and market demand, write down your findings in a one page document. Brainstorm all of your ideas first; then produce a concise picture of your Big Idea. This will form an integral part of the business plan that you will compile in section four. In the next chapter, we look at how to use the basis of this information to turn your Big Idea into a viable, tangible product.

7

How can you turn your Big Idea into a product?

The next stage is to transform your Big Idea into a viable, tangible product. That means taking all that you have learned and developed and applying it to develop a finished item. The finished item may still be a prototype at this stage if more research and development

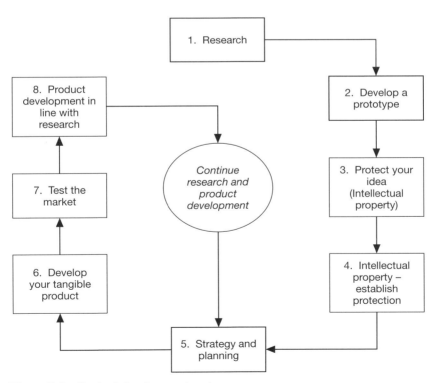

Figure 7.1 Product development cycle

is required, but it's important to have developed the framework for your product in order to move it forward. The eight steps illustrated in figure 7.1 should be followed when entering into product development.

We will focus on step six in this section. Let's assume for now that the necessary research has been carried out, you have any patents required and that your product sends a clear strategic message. The next step in the process is to develop a prototype version of your Big Idea.

A prototype is the first sample product to be made and should be viewed as a starting point for advancement, so it pays to start thinking about its initial development now. It helps to have a prototype product to work with when researching, developing a marketing strategy, determining patent rights and certainly for strategic planning.

Should you find a manufacturer or can you do it yourself?

Depending on what your Big Idea is, you might choose to develop and create a prototype product yourself or with the help of friends. This can be a cost saving and time effective method that will ensure the product is produced exactly to your specific requirements. A word of warning however: make sure the prototype is good quality. The last thing you want is to go in front of an investor with a product that falls apart or fails to do the job for which it was intended. You will rarely be given a second chance to present your business proposal to the same investor.

The alternative is to find a manufacturer who can mock up a prototype to your specifications. You will save time, money and energy if you can be as specific as possible about the detail of your product. Provide the manufacturer with detailed drawings and designs that are to scale. If the manufactured prototype does not meet your requirements, don't be afraid to keep modifying the product in discussion with the manufacturer until it is absolutely right. Getting a perfect prototype product (based on the information and research you have done at this stage) could either impress or deter future banks, investors, customers or other interested parties.

The Department of Trade and Industry can provide useful information on developing a product to prototype stage. However, the best resource I have found in recent years is the Internet, which may lead you to discover that the best market for sourcing raw materials is overseas, for example in China. While it may be the most cost effective method of generating a prototype, do make sure that sourcing products abroad fits with the ethos or message of your product and company.

Developing a prototype can be exciting as it may be the first time your Big Idea has taken a tangible form. Take your time and make sure it reflects, as closely as possible, the dream you have for your Big Idea. Test the product in real situations to make sure it will stand up under scrutiny. Now that you have your product, it's time to give it a name.

What's in a name?

What do you currently call your Big Idea? Is it the intended name for the product? Don't worry about the company name at this stage; we'll cover that issue in section six of the book. For now, focus on your product and the message that you want to give customers. You may decide to change or develop the name once more market research is carried out, but for now it's important to label your prototype product for maximum impact.

Take some time to think about your product name and its suitability for the market by answering the following questions:

1. Who are you trying to appeal to? Will they expect plain speech or be drawn in by conceptual jargon?

2. What does your product actually do? Is this reflected in the name, either practically or conceptually? For example, an airline called Airways would be practical, whereas one called Blue would be conceptual (as in 'blue sky' ideas).

3. How does it translate? If you know your markets are to be the UK, France and Spain, make sure your name doesn't translate badly into French or Spanish.

4. Has the name been used before? Trawl the Internet and search for previous uses of your chosen product name. It is also useful to read relevant trade journals to make sure the name is not too similar to an existing product, especially if the product is similar to yours.

Is it more appropriate to have a practical or a conceptual name? Think about the product, its uses and your target customer base. Would purchasers be more likely to buy a new style lawn mower called 'Green Field' or 'Easy-Mow'? The general rule is that if the function of the product is practical, the name should reflect its purpose. There are many exceptions to this rule, however having to explain the concept and your product name can be difficult and costly. Education of the market is expensive.

Some interesting examples of appropriate product names and where they came from are:

Volvo – From the Latin for *I roll*, which was appropriate as Volvo started out as a ball bearings company.

LEGO – From the Danish word *leg godt* meaning to play well.

Sony – From the Latin word *son*, meaning sound.

Nivea – From the Latin word *niveus*, meaning snowy white.

Being creative with the product name can result in a unique and interesting product name that still sums up what the product is designed to do.

Don't forget to check for any hidden meanings or translations of your product name, especially if you are planning to sell to international markets, and make sure the name doesn't change in translation to mean something else; or worse, something offensive. One example of a product name that has been lost in translation is Brillo. Originally the brand name derived from a simple abbreviation of the word 'brilliant'; but in Italian *brillo* means drunk or tipsy. Imagine the Italians buying the misnamed cleaning product to scrub pots and pans. If you are hoping or likely to trade in a country where the first language is not English, ask someone who speaks the language to check your brand name.

Conclusion

Developing a product from your Big Idea can be an intensely personal and rewarding experience. You will finally see your dream become a tangible product with which to grow your new business. Throughout this process, keep focused on what you are trying to achieve – develop a prototype product that is as close as possible to your specifications and that is appropriately and interestingly named. This prototype may change after you have further researched and developed your concept, but for now this is your flagship product, so make sure it works and embodies your Big Idea.

Key points to remember

If you don't yet have a Big Idea, answer the following questions:

▶ What do you know about?

▶ What experiences have you had?

▶ What do you want to do?

▶ Do any products on the market bother you or someone else you know?

Understand the detail of your Big Idea and learn to communicate the concept effectively.

Define your Big Idea in one sentence that will start to answer the following questions:

▶ What does the product do?

▶ Why is it better than anything else on the market?

▶ How does the product work?

▶ Why will it help the user?

▶ Is it affordable?

▶ What is your Big Idea's unique selling point (USP)?

Now is the time to start market research to make sure others share your enthusiasm. Be open to constructive criticism and try to build this into further product development. Product development should be an ongoing process incorporating feedback on the initial proto-type. Choose the right brand name for your product by answering the following questions:

- ▶ Who are you trying to appeal to with your product?
- ▶ What does your product actually do?
- ▶ How does your name translate into foreign markets or into slang?
- ▶ Has the name been used before?

Research and Marketing

Now that you have a firm grasp of the integrity of your Big Idea, it is time to research the product and its market in greater detail. Thorough research at this stage is integral to moving forward with confidence in what you are selling, understanding why you are selling it, and to whom you intend to sell your product. The marketing profession is wide and full of experts who may give you conflicting advice on how best to market your product. This section of the book will provide the techniques proven to help small businesses identify and target their chosen market.

Chapter 8 – How should you approach market research?

Research should provide you with the answer to any question that may be asked about your product by an investor, a customer, a supplier, an employee or any other interested party. It is important to prepare as much information as you can about your Big Idea and how it will operate in a business environment before setting up your company. Thorough research now will save you time and money later.

Use market analysis to identify, test and analyse the target market for your product. The information that can be gained from the prospective customer base is invaluable when refining your product and deciding how to bring it to market. Make sure you understand your market and the behaviour of your target customer base.

Chapter 9 – What do you need to know about marketing before you start?

Marketing is crucial for small business success. There is a wide range of approaches to marketing, many of which can be expensive and/or ineffective. It is important that you know the marketing options available and use these to determine which method is appropriate for your specific product. Understand the basics of marketing and harness the power that focused, concentrated marketing techniques can bring to a small business.

8

How should you approach market research?

The key to understanding your market is to first understand your product. Market analysis and how to market your product are explained later in this chapter and also in chapter nine, but first we will focus on the product that has been developed from your Big Idea. The value of research into your product should not be underestimated. Getting to know the detail of your product, its type and its complete functionality will help you unlock its full potential. But where do you start to collect information and how will you know the value of good research data?

Data collection and its value

Thanks to the advent of the Internet, there is a wealth of information on any topic now available at our finger tips; but remember that much of it is unverified data, which can mislead and confuse the reader. When collecting data for research make sure it is from a verified, reliable source to ensure business decisions are based on fact not conjecture. Before collecting research data, you must determine two things:

1. What questions do you want the research to answer?
2. What are likely sources of valuable, genuine and reliable information?

Research questions

When embarking on research, your approach should be targeted and focused. The best way to approach this is to use research to answer specific questions about your product and the market in which you intend to operate. Some questions you may want answered include:

▶ Will there be demand for my product?

▶ What similar products are on the market?

▶ How much should I charge for my product?

▶ Are the features of my product good enough to create demand?

▶ Why do customers buy the products they buy?

▶ Who will buy my product?

▶ How can I make my product for less while keeping the desired level of quality?

▶ What's the best way to package my product?

▶ How will I deliver my product to market?

▶ Do I need to set up a shop, sell via the Internet or should I sell through other companies?

The list of questions could go on and on. The above list contains questions that almost everyone embarking on setting up a company should be asking themselves at this stage. There will be more specific questions based on the nature of your product and industry, so take some time to compile your own list of questions. Your research will then have a focus.

Data sources

Market research can range from free information to expensive data compiled by a third party. There is no reason why you cannot collect sufficient data to answer the questions above by doing some legwork for a minimal cost, if not for free. If you have specific information requirements, such as scientific research data, you may need to collect data from a specific source that will require payment for their services. Try to get as much data from public information as possible, as there is a lot of data available that will answer the majority of questions without breaking the bank prior to set-up.

Some possible data sources for research include:

▶ The Internet (beware of the integrity of the data).

▶ Department of Trade and Industry (DTI).

▶ Local government – many councils run small business initiatives.

▶ Banks – many high street banks can offer market analysis and statistics to their clients.

▶ Trade bodies – can provide important information on standards and regulatory requirements.

▶ Industry magazines – provide information on companies, products and key individuals within an industry.

▶ Trade shows – see your competition and their products in action to determine how popular and dynamic they are.

▶ Companies operating in the industry – direct approaches are quite often the best way to collect data for research, though often the most difficult as companies tend to be guarded about performance unless they are doing very well. Bear in mind that this type of research may only provide one side of the story, as companies will generally tell you what they are doing well, not what lessons they have learned.

These data sources can be tied into your question list as follows:

Question	Data source	Desired research output
What similar products are on the market?	Retail outlets, trade shows, the Internet.	Product name, retail price, list of common characteristics of each product; list of unique selling points of each product and how they are marketed.
Who will buy my product?	Trade shows, DTI, local government, consumer groups.	Customer profile of likely individuals or groups who will purchase your product.
What's the best way to package my product?	Retailers or wholesalers, consumers, government.	Statutory guidelines regarding packaging and labelling of your type of product; retailers' expectations of packaging (for presentation or due to shelf space limitations); determine what appeals to customers.

There are many ways to go about collecting data to answer your research questions. Ensure that the data you collect is reliable and is timely. Consumer tastes can change, especially regarding products involving technology or gimmicks, so make sure you keep your research up to date and use sources that reflect the wider market.

Activity: How to apply market research data

Consider one of your most pressing questions. For example, an important question usually asked at this stage is, 'How much should be charged for the product?' The pricing of a product reflects the image that you wish to project as well as its contribution to the profitability of the company. The mechanics of how to approach pricing is covered in chapter nine, but for now focus on collecting the data.

Follow the four steps as outlined below in this basic, but effective, market research activity. The example of pricing a product in the luxury goods market has been used as an example throughout the activity.

1. Determine the image of your product. Is it to be perceived as a luxury item, or should it be made available to the wider market?

2. If, for example, you are targeting the luxury market, go to all of the retail outlets who sell your type of product at the top end of the market. Note down the price of each product, its characteristics, its packaging and how it is displayed. Ask yourself why each product is perceived as a luxury item. Why would you pay more for one product than another similar but cheaper product?

3. Use the Internet, trade magazines or industry suppliers to determine the significance of ingredients, components or the method of preparation that make each luxury product stand out. Corporate advertising will quite often provide some answers, but beware of exaggerated claims and statements made to entice customers, as they can often be misleading when you want pure, empirical evidence and plenty of facts. Having an understanding of why some products are priced differently from other products which seem similar is essential to understanding the make-up of your own product.

4. Consider your product against a list of similar products. Make sure that your product stacks up against the competition. If it is similar in quality to the luxury items, then pricing for the top end of the market should be justified. Don't forget that customers paying for luxury goods are charged a premium for the brand as well as for the product itself. As a start-up, you are unlikely to have any brand presence or goodwill, so you may have to price your product competitively against more established brands, despite having produced a similar quality of product.

Once you've completed this activity, ask yourself the following question. Have the results of the research changed how you view any aspect of your product or how you intend to market it? The application of research results can sometimes be confusing as it can be difficult to see how this new information could impact on what you have already achieved. Be open to change as new information could highlight areas of weakness to improve upon or areas of strengths upon which to capitalise.

Use market research to maximise the potential of your product

Any information gained from the data sources listed above should be documented and used to maximise the potential of your product. At this pre-launch stage you have the opportunity to make changes to your product, whereas it is very difficult to modify your product, its price, packaging or marketing after you have launched, as you may risk confusing, or even alienating your customers. Add your own product specification to the list of competing products that you created during the above activity. Be critical about how your product compares with the rest. Now take your observations a step further and ask yourself how you can make your product better than, or different from the competition.

Don't be afraid to stand out from the crowd. Often a significant differentiator is what it takes for a new entrant to attract customer attention. Many small companies, that cannot afford expensive advertising campaigns, have made the mistake of replicating a product already on the market. Do something different. Your product will need to stand up and speak for itself.

Customer profiling

Once you are happy that your product is exactly right for the market at this time, think about who will buy it. Who are your customers? Hopefully your research will have shed some light on what your ideal customer base might be. It is useful at this stage to generate a customer profile. This gives your customer an identity. Some people will go so far as to give their imaginary customer a name as well, in order to really 'get to know' their market. Do what feels right for you. This can seem like a frivolous exercise, but it does work when it comes to focusing attention on how to sell and market the product. Generate a separate customer identity profile for each different product.

Use the template below to provide the answers that will generate the information needed to produce a customer profile.

Who are your customers?	
Where do your customers live?	
Where do they shop?	
What is important to your customer?	
How much disposable income do they have?	
How much are they likely to be able to afford, or want to spend on this product?	

A customer identity profile might be represented as follows:

Product	
'Name'	
Age	
Education	
Ethnic/religious background	
Hobbies	
Monthly spending habits	
Monthly disposable income	
Method of purchasing	

Now that you have your customer profile, how do you go about finding your target customers? Generate some market analysis to identify your target market. Make sure you are communicating with the people who you have identified as your target market.

Market research

You now know who is going to buy your product, but how do you find out where they are? Conducting some market research at this stage will identify your target market and help you understand how to communicate to them your message about your product.

How to find your target market

Don't make the assumption that everyone will want to buy your product. The reality is that a small percentage of the total population will be interested enough to part with their hard-earned cash to buy what you are selling. Before you develop a marketing strategy, you must be able to identify and locate your target market. Don't try to be all things to all people. This strategy is doomed to fail in the vast majority of cases. Aim your product at a select group of people – your target market. Understanding that customers are motivated to spend for three basic reasons can help focus your marketing efforts. Customers' motives for purchasing include:

1. To satisfy their basic requirements.
2. To solve a problem.
3. To make themselves happy.

Identify which of these motives your product will satisfy. It is possible that your product will meet more than one of these purchasing criteria. For example, a bakery offering sweet pastries can satisfy basic hunger and can also make the customer happy as the product can be considered a treat.

Use the customer profile outline on page 71 to define your target market through market segmentation. Use public information to find your chosen segment of the market. Local governments and the Department of Trade and Industry have information that will help you do this. Answering the following questions will also help you locate these precious perspective customers:

▶ Where are they likely to shop?

▶ Where are they likely to engage in leisure pursuits?

▶ Where are their children likely to go to school?

▶ Where are they likely to dine out?

▶ Where are they likely to live?

▶ What other products are they likely to purchase?

Your research has indicated that your customer profile is likely to be a 32-year-old middle-class mother. Think about what she does during the day: going to playgroups, supermarkets, retail outlets, cafes. Where is she going to be? Try to think like your customer – put yourself in her shoes. This logic can be applied to any customer profile, to help determine your target market and their location for targeted marketing.

Market analysis

Market analysis simply tests what your target market thinks and feels about your product. The key is to use this information for more effective marketing and to hone your product's specifications to ensure that it will sell and provide you with a profit.

Now that your customer profile has been established, find a population sample that reflects the entire population of your target market. This can be a small group of around 10-20 people; but if resources allow, a larger group of up to 100 participants will result in a better cross-section of data. Try to obtain a cross-section within the customer profile if possible. For example, if your profile indicates your target market is 25-year-old professional males, try to include people from a wide range of professions and backgrounds. Use the sample population to test your product with some basic market analysis. You could select your sample population by approaching people in the identified market locations, asking friends and family, advertising for willing participants (generally by offering something for free) or by using pre-existing data.

A word of warning: while using pre-existing data is the cheapest and quickest way to collect information for market analysis, there is no way of knowing just how relevant and accurate it is, so use the information in conjunction with other research collected by a verifiable source.

Conclusion

You don't need to pay a fortune to obtain some initial market research. Once you have a clear idea of what your Big Idea is, tell your friends, family and anyone who'll listen. Get their honest feedback and make sure you keep plenty of notes as you will draw on this information in the future. Be careful though. If another budding entrepreneur gets wind of your Big Idea they may want to run with it themselves, so be selective and choose to involve only people you trust.

If you feel you need a broader cross-section of opinion, you can do independent research using previously collected and reported statistics. You can also move on to some more formal market research of your own, focusing specifically on your Big Idea. There are many agencies that will generate a survey to gauge popular opinion on a range of topics. Remember to be adaptable. Don't be so fixed on your Big Idea that you can't adapt it in response to feedback that you receive. Even if what you hear initially sounds too risky or just not what you had planned, it is worth taking on board what people say. Apply their logic to your Big Idea to see whether it can be improved, before you move to the next stage of your business planning.

CHAPTER NINE

What do you need to know about marketing?

Now that you have carried out your market research, you should learn and understand the basics of marketing before you move on to financial planning. This chapter will cover the marketing techniques applied by marketing and advertising agencies to both large and small companies.

The purpose of marketing is to deliver your product to the customer efficiently and profitably. Marketing aims to put the right product at the right price in the right place at the right time, so that it appeals to the right person. You don't need to be a seasoned marketer to get this concept right and make it work for your company. There are many ways to market your product without hiring expensive agencies to do the job for you.

Understanding the buying decision

In chapter eight, you established the identity of your customer by completing the customer profile activity. However, there are also other individuals, groups and factors to consider when developing your marketing strategy. While the actual purchase is made by your customer, the buying process can also be influenced by the following factors:

> ▶ *Initiators* – individuals who first suggest the concept for a particular product. For example a colleague may suggest a product that would solve the complaint of a fellow worker.

> ▶ *Influencers* – a person or group who may influence the decision to make the purchase. For example, an influential advertising campaign may feature a convincing celebrity figure.

> ▶ *Deciders* – the person who makes the decision to purchase the product. This may be the customer himself or the person in control of the customer's finances.

> ▶ *Buyers* – the person who physically makes the purchase. The decider and buyer can often be different parties. For example, limited access may restrict the decider's ability to make the purchase.

> ▶ *Users* – the end-user of the product may not participate in any part of the buying process and yet their anticipated reaction to the product may be a factor in the motivation to purchase. For example, a child's likely reaction to a toy could become an influencer in future purchasing activity.

Your marketing strategy, where possible, should consider all of the parties involved in the buying decision, with the decider being at the core of the process.

The marketing mix (the 4 Ps)

When considering which marketing tools to use, the marketing mix is a good place to start. Including a mix of the following four categories (the 4 Ps) should ensure that you cover every aspect of marketing your product efficiently and effectively.

> ▶ *Product* – what is the specification of the product?

> ▶ *Price* – how much should you charge for the product?

> ▶ *Place* – where should you sell the product?

> ▶ *Promotion* – how can you tell people about the product?

Each of the components in the marketing mix is interlinked and the common theme of the product should run through each component consistently. For example, if your price is targeting the luxury market, then your product should be good enough to support this strategy. Product placement should be at a luxury outlet and the promotion should be targeting those with a sufficiently high level of disposable income.

The following sections explain each of these points in turn. They form a logical process to follow when applying marketing to a small business – see figure 9.1.

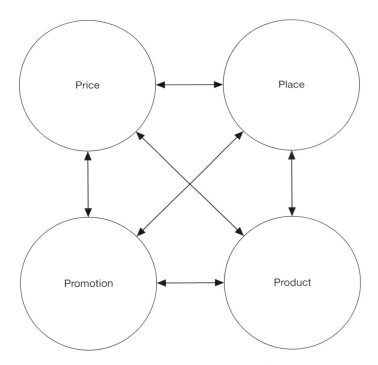

Figure 9.1   The marketing mix is also known as the 4 Ps

Product

Your product is made up of a whole package of benefits aimed at the customer. By the time you are planning your marketing mix you should have completed your market research to ensure that your product is wanted in the market. Use this stage before the launch of your business to further refine your product and make sure you stay up-to-date with market demand and expectations.

Consider the following factors when preparing your product for market:

- ▶ Quality
- ▶ Size
- ▶ Styling
- ▶ Packaging
- ▶ Functionality
- ▶ Safety
- ▶ Brand
- ▶ Support

Your product should stand up to scrutiny based on the above points. While some people can sell anything, it is true for most of us that we sell more effectively if we have confidence in what we are communicating. Keep comparing and contrasting your product with other products on the market and above all, make sure you know your product intimately so you can maximise the benefit of your marketing strategy.

Price

There are many factors to consider when deciding on the price of a product. The three most important ones however are: what your customer can afford (or is willing to pay); what your competitors charge; and your expected level of profitability. If you are able to quantify these three factors they will give you a range within which you will find the logical retail price of your product.

Mike wants to determine a retail price for his bespoke furniture, specifically a table that he has designed. He has identified his target market and determined that a customer is likely to pay up to £1000 for a table of similar specification. He must charge at least £700 to make a profit. Competing products on the market range from £800 to £1200 in price; therefore his optimal retail price should fall within the range of £700 to £1000.

Your customers' buying decision is likely to be influenced by price factors, so research your target market sufficiently well to establish what people are willing to pay for your product. It is essential that your product should be within the affordability range of your target market.

Consider the following factors when determining the appropriate price for your product:

▶ Retail price

▶ Pricing strategy

▶ Level of disposable income of your target market

▶ Distribution and retailer mark-up

▶ Discounts (retail or wholesale)

▶ Seasonal pricing

A retail price is a starting point. Bear in mind that, as a new entrant, you may need to offer your product at a discount to attract initial interest in the product (known as introductory pricing). Many small companies also use distributors instead of an internal sales force; this is often very cost effective (the issue of distribution is covered in more detail in section five). However, external sales and distribution forces are likely to want to negotiate for a percentage of the retail price, which will result in a reduction in your profits or an increase in the retail price.

Place

Ensure that customers can buy your product easily, and with minimal disruption to their lives. This is even more important in the new era of online shopping. We all want easy access to products and product information. Make sure your customers don't have to try too hard to find you.

Placement of your product is critical, regardless of the type or level of promotional activity. While product promotion is an important factor for spreading the word, it's vital that, once the customer decides to make the purchase, they can find the product easily and from a reliable source.

The following factors are important considerations when determining the placement of your product:

- ▶ Distributors
- ▶ Warehousing – stock control, lead times, availability
- ▶ Logistics – order processing
- ▶ Market coverage
- ▶ Retail or wholesale outlets
- ▶ Sales territories

Promotion

There are many ways in which you can reach your target market, but beware – advertising and marketing activities are costly – so do ensure that you are targeting the people who are most likely to want to buy your product. You should consider the following factors when determining the placement of your product:

- ▶ Public relations (PR)
- ▶ Sales force – who and why?
- ▶ Sales promotion

► Advertising
► Direct marketing

Advertising is generally very expensive in terms of air time or print space; and the use of an advertising agency to conceptualise and generate an advertisement will also stretch your budget. As your product is likely to be untested, it is worth waiting until you have a better understanding of your target market and their purchasing behaviour before choosing to launch an advertising campaign.

You can reach your market very effectively without the use of expensive advertising. Some marketing options available to the small business include:

► Direct mail
► Cold calling
► Complementary marketing
► Advertorials and interviews

Direct mail

Direct mail refers to anything that you send in the post; such as letters, brochures or mail-outs. For direct mail to be successful, you must understand the recipient. A two per cent response rate for this style of marketing is considered to be good. However, it is dangerous to assume that a fixed percentage of recipients will reply. The response rate will depend upon the number of people who glance at or even read direct mail. It will also depend on your product, its price point and its suitability to the reader. Do a test mail-out of say 500 mailers first, and hope for around ten responses. This should prevent overspend on a method that doesn't often work for small businesses who can't afford significant market research. Personalised mailings tend to be more successful than those addressed to 'the occupant'. For the most effective results, consider renting a named, up-to-date mailing list from a known company that offers a complementary service to your own.

Cold calling

Use the criteria you have gathered about your target market to identify and build a database of contact names and numbers. Use this information to spread the word about your product yourself. Call potential retailers to ask if they will stock your product, as well as potential customers who have been identified as likely purchasers of your product. While time consuming, this is often an effective way to reach your first customers. Make sure that you are speaking to a decision-maker in the company rather than an office junior, and if the answer is negative remain positive and say that you'll keep in touch. Don't take 'No's' at face value. Every call you make is a step towards building another useful business relationship.

Complementary marketing

A cost effective and efficient way of reaching your target market is by teaming up with a company that is selling a complementary product. For example, if your company produces slate flooring, getting a kitchen building company to agree to recommend your business would be an ideal way to provide access to the perfect target market.

Advertorials and interviews

Call local magazines and newspapers to let them know you are about to launch an exciting new product and business. Editors are often interested in doing pieces on local residents who are providing something new and interesting to their readers. You should also set your sights higher than solely the local market, though it could be more difficult to establish a news link that will convince an editor further afield to allocate precious column inches to your product.

Think of any interesting – and relevant – facts about yourself or your product that customers might be interested in. The trick then is to find a suitable publication that will be willing to publish your story. Don't forget to continue to focus on appealing to your target market; free press coverage can do more harm than good if it sends out the wrong message.

Activity: Applying the marketing mix

Think about your product and start to apply the marketing mix as a model for developing a marketing strategy. Create a draft plan, using each of the 4 Ps as a heading, to ensure that you have continuity as you take your message to the market. It is easy to send mixed messages, so mapping out your strategy now using the format below should help to focus your message at this early stage.

Product name and target market	Product	Price	Placement	Promotion
Product type A: Target market – brief description.	Detailed product specification.	Retail price and pricing strategy. (Is this a high-, middle- or low-end product?)	Based on price, where do you intend to place the product to attract the market you are targeting?	Where do you expect to find your target market and how do you intend to speak to them?

Repeat the above activity for each separate product that you intend to launch to the market. Make sure you are focusing on the same target market throughout each area of your marketing strategy.

The importance of a website

The use of a website is worthy of separate comment. In today's commercial and technological environment many consumers use the Internet to research and compare products and to make their purchases. Most of us expect a product to have a web presence of some form. Some options for the small business owner are as follows:

▶ Develop your own website

▶ Use a retailer's website

▶ Add reviews to a commercial website

▶ Monitor your web presence

Develop your own website

A website doesn't have to be expensive or complicated. It is worth registering a domain name (web address) for your company or product name as soon as possible. If your specific name is taken, try different variations, such as incorporating an underscore, a hyphen, or the word 'online' as part of the address; or opt for '.co.uk', or '.net' instead of '.com' as the suffix.

Keep trying various options until a web address becomes available; just don't become too obscure or stray too far from the actual product name. Many products require only a simple website, listing information about the product and including contact details for further information. This type of website can be generated using a generic software package or online template; or can be developed by a professional for as little as £500. Taking your website to the next level by allowing purchasing activity will require further development and the facility to take payment via a secure means, using a company such as PayPal. Your bank may also be able to offer a cash handling facility and may be able to offer very helpful advice. Finalising a website can be a protracted process, so if you are planning to sell via the Internet, start by looking into what facilities your bank and other institutions may offer to help you take cash payments online.

Use a retailer's website

An alternative method, if you wish to trade online yet do not wish to set this feature up for yourself, is to use a retailer's website for Internet purchasing activity. This involves placing your product on a retailer's website or marketplace website. There will normally be a commission payable to the retailer, either per transaction or a percentage of sales value. This method can be a simple and cost-effective way of selling your product online during the early stages of the product's life.

Add reviews to a commercial website

Customers will often use the Internet to research and compare products before making a purchase, and they read reviews on commercial websites. This is as true of low-value products, such as mascara, as it is of high-end purchases, such as a car. Once you have a product, try to arrange for some reviews to appear on relevant websites, even before launch; though ideally the reviews should be timed to coincide with the launch of your product in order to create initial interest.

Monitor your web presence

Once you have started to establish your product, or have launched your website, try logging on to Google (www.google.com) periodically to search for your product name and product type. See how many results are returned. This exercise is useful for keeping an eye on your competitors and customers' expectations of your type of product. It will also show what level of presence you have on the web. If online selling is to be an essential part of your business it may be worth finding out the cost of subscribing to an efficient search engine to help raise your corporate profile.

Conclusion

Marketing can seem a complex and confusing area for the small-business owner but it needn't be. Keep your marketing message simple; do your research and make sure you are sending a consistent message throughout all your communications to the market as a whole as well as to your target customer base.

Use the 4 Ps as your framework to focus your mind on which aspects of your product are the most important. Don't forget that the 4 Ps are called the marketing *mix*. They are mixed together to create a consistent marketing strategy; so ensure that the same message is at the heart of each of the product, price, placement and promotion strategies.

3

Key points to remember

Market research can be carried out through data collected by using the following questions:

- ▶ Will there be demand for my product?
- ▶ What similar products are on the market?
- ▶ How much should I charge for my product?
- ▶ Are the features of my product good enough to create demand?
- ▶ Why do customers buy the products they buy?
- ▶ Who will buy my product?
- ▶ How can I make my product for less, while keeping the desired level of quality?
- ▶ What's the best way to package my product?
- ▶ How will I deliver my product to market?
- ▶ Do I need to set up a shop, use the Internet, or should I sell via other companies?

Consider the following data sources when collecting your market research data:

- ▶ The Internet
- ▶ Department of Trade and Industry (DTI)
- ▶ Local government
- ▶ Banks
- ▶ Trade bodies
- ▶ Industry magazines

▶ Trade shows

▶ Companies operating in the industry

Customer profiling will help you to understand your market and aid in product development. Answering the following questions will help to define your target customer profile:

▶ Who is your ideal customer?

▶ Where do your customers live?

▶ Where do your customers shop?

▶ What is important to your customer?

▶ How much disposable income does your customer have?

▶ How much are they likely to spend on a similar product?

Use marketing techniques to understand the buying decision, which is influenced by the following parties:

▶ Initiators

▶ Influencers

▶ Deciders

▶ Buyers

▶ Users

The key to your marketing strategy is the marketing mix (the 4 Ps), which is made up of the following:

▶ *Product* – what is the specification of your product?

▶ *Price* – how much should I charge for the product?

▶ *Place* – where should I sell the product?

▶ *Promotion* – how can I tell people about the product?

Business Planning

Every start-up company requires a business plan, which will incorporate all the commercial and financial aspects of your proposed business. This section of the book will guide you through the essential components of a business plan and explains how to find the information and how to put it all together in a clear concise format. The chapters also explore how you intend to finance the business and address some common pitfalls that occur at this stage of the process.

Chapter 10 – How do you create a business plan?

Creating a business plan is an important exercise for any small business owner, and you will undoubtedly learn a lot about your product and what is expected from an operating business in the process. Not only is preparing a business plan vital for focusing your attention on what is important in a business, it is also an essential document for showing to key people who need to see a comprehensive summary of the business, such as banks and investors.

Chapter 11 – What do you include in the financial section of the business plan?

The financial section of the business plan must make financial sense to any reader and must be clear as to how the business plans to make money. Information about sales volume, retail price, discounts, direct costs and overheads should be included, to calculate the profit for the business. Cashflow should also be reported, as it will be important for you and any potential investor to understand your cash requirements and how any cash injection is likely to be used. A balance sheet, used to report the assets and liabilities of the company, is also included in this section.

Chapter 12 – How should you finance the business?

You should have an awareness of the financial options and third parties available to you to seek finance for your business. There is a wide range of private individuals and institutions available to assist in supporting your business, so be aware of who they are, how to contact them and what their objectives and requirements are.

Chapter 13 – What are the common pitfalls of business?

Understanding the common pitfalls of business can help the small business owner anticipate any problems that may arise before they happen. Learn from others' mistakes and try to avoid the common problems that can harm small business activity.

10

How do you create a business plan?

In this chapter we will look at the reasons why you should create a business plan, how to go about producing a business plan and what to do with the document once it has been created. Now is the time

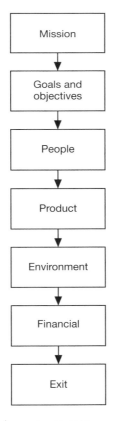

Figure 10.1 Business planning process map

to start thinking of your Big Idea as an operational business if you don't already. There is a big difference between having a great idea and having a business that actually makes financial and commercial sense.

The market and product research you carried out in previous chapters will be used in the process of compiling the business plan, along with new information about your team (covered in full in section five); and financial information, which we will cover in this chapter (See figure 10.1).

Why create a business plan?

The purpose of a business plan is for you and for other people to understand the business and how it is going to make money. While there are many components in a business plan, it is wise to keep them simple. There is no need to overcomplicate your business plan at this or any stage of your business.

The business plan is your chance to make sure your product will generate sufficient income and profits to become a viable business. The process of a planning activity often highlights areas of weakness that can then be resolved before the launch of the company.

The owners of small businesses often become so close to their Big Idea, product or company strategy, that they find it difficult to articulate their plans to a third party who has little knowledge of the product or industry. A clear, concise business plan should act to translate relevant business information to interested third parties, such as banks, investors, future employees and suppliers. It should also answer questions and put people's minds at ease as to the viability of your business offering.

How detailed do my plans need to be?

The level of detail that you need to put into your business plan will depend on your business. Generally speaking, the more detailed the plan, the better prepared a company will be for any eventuality, whether planned or a surprise. However, there is sometimes a fine line between a detailed plan and a complex one. Keeping a business plan simple is always a good approach, so try to keep detail clear and concise.

I have often been told by investors that they will not look at a business plan if it is longer than ten pages, but any shorter than that may result in information and detail being missed out. So as a general rule of thumb, a ten-page business plan is sufficient at this stage of your new venture. You can always provide further breakdown of information if specifically requested. These ten pages should cover the seven sections as detailed below and in figure 10.1. The key sections of your business plan are:

▶ Mission statement   page 1
▶ Goals and objectives   page 2
▶ Key management team   page 3
▶ Product   pages 4–5
▶ Environmental analysis   pages 6–7
▶ Financial summary   pages 8–9
▶ Exit strategy   page 10

There is a lot of information to consider when creating your business plan, but don't feel you have to include every detail. The key is to consider every area of your business and consolidate your data clearly and concisely. The main points listed above should always be included in a business plan of any new company in its early stages. Let's look at each of these points individually:

Mission statement

Your mission statement should be a short, concise message about what you hope to achieve through your product and the company. The message will be used in your business plan as well as in marketing information, so make it something that will appeal to a wide audience. It needn't be too specific or detailed at this point. An example of a mission statement might be:

'To be the leader in childcare nurseries in the Greater London area.'

Think about what this statement means. There are three important components to this mission statement:

Leader – what does this mean to you? Does this mean to become the leader in terms of number of children, the most profit, or provision of the best or most unique educational experience? The term leader can mean different things to different people – make sure you know what it means to you.

Childcare nurseries – there are many types of childcare nurseries and they use several different styles of curriculum. Make sure you are clear about the different types of nurseries, the differences in teaching style, the services they offer and how you intend to provide your specific product. In other words, be sure about what you are offering and to whom.

Greater London – be clear about what this geographical reference means. If you claim to be the leader in a large area, make sure your plans cover the whole of the district and not just the south-west postcodes, for example. Nor should you go to the other extreme by stating that you plan to branch out into the surrounding counties in year two. It's fine to have the ambition to do this, but it is important that your business plan is synchronised with your mission statement.

The following are mission statements of successful, international companies:

▶ The Walt Disney Company has an environmental mission statement, which reads as follows:

'The Walt Disney Company is committed to balancing environmental stewardship with its corporate goals and operations throughout the world.'

While this is an admirable sentiment, it doesn't really say that much as we don't know what the corporate goals are and therefore what the environmental stewardship is to be balanced against.

▶ Ford UK has a mission statement that capitalises on its history, with a focus on product quality:

'We are a global, diverse family with a proud heritage, passionately committed to providing outstanding products and services.'

This mission statement is very well worded. In just one sentence, Ford has summed up many aspects of the company: global, diverse, history, enthusiasm, product quality, service quality.

Try to find some mission statements of companies you admire and analyse what they consider to be important enough about their business to mention in the brief mission statement.

Goals and objectives

Your business plan should briefly describe the goals and objectives of the company. It is important that the person reading the business plan understands where you hope to take the company and how you intend to get there.

We looked at your personal and business goals and objectives in chapter two. It is now time to ensure that these goals and objectives are realistic and reflect accurately what you hope to achieve through this endeavour. Choose your top three goals and objectives to clarify your purpose. These should flow naturally from the sentiment of your mission statement. It is also worth providing a brief outline as to what action you intend to take to meet these goals and objectives. Again, just a brief explanation is sufficient for this summary level of introductory information. The following table represents an example of common goals and objectives and a brief comment on how they might be achieved.

Goals and objectives	How this will be achieved
To capture a niche market in the telecoms industry.	Through partnering with companies that are proven in the market and which provide a complementary product.
To make 15 per cent profit from year one.	By charging an aggressive sales price due to our unique selling point; combined with tight control of direct costs and overheads.
To provide a unique product to the frozen food market.	Our research will enable us to develop a product with a sufficiently unique selling point (USP) that it will appeal to customers so that they will move away from their existing product to take up this new product offering. By maintaining current knowledge of competitor behaviour to ensure the USP is retained.

Key management team

Your key management team should be outlined with a brief biography for each person – including yourself. Incorporate relevant information about academic achievements and work experience as well as career highlights, membership of trade bodies and why each individual is part of the team.

You should ensure that your key management team spans the main processes and areas of the company – strategic, operational and financial. It is fine for one person to take on more than one of these functions, but make it clear that this is the case so that the reader can feel comfortable that all areas of the company have a dedicated key manager.

Product

Use the results of the research activities carried out in chapter eight to answer the following questions about your product:

1. What is it?

2. What is it called?

3. What does it do?

4. How is it different from everything else on the market?

5. Why will people buy it?

6. How will people buy it?

7. How much will it cost?

Use these seven questions as a guide to the information required for your product page. You could also include a picture or drawings of the product, though these should be referenced on the product page and included in the appendix. Make sure the reader will understand why your product will appeal to the market from the two pages you have available to give them this message.

Environmental analysis

Use the market and competitor information from section three to complete the environmental analysis summary. Figures 10.2 and 10.3 list the features of two types of business analysis: the PEST (political, economic, social and technological) and SWOT (strengths, weaknesses, opportunities and threats) formats are management techniques for gathering and analysing data for business planning. Both formats are useful. Take some time to think about the issues relevant to your product and your proposed business that might fit into each section of the PEST and SWOT analysis tables.

Financial summary

The financial summary will be covered in further detail in chapter 11, but in this section we will look at the component parts of the financial summary pages. The basic information required for the financial summary page is as follows:

▶ Product profitability and sales volume assumptions.

▶ Profit and loss statement – year one detail.

Political	Economic
Issues such as:	*Issues such as:*
• Intellectual property protection • Pricing regulations • Taxation • Product labelling requirements	• Labour costs • Interest rates • Exchange rates • Inflation rates
Social	**Technological**
Issues such as:	*Issues such as:*
• Demographics • Education • Culture • Leisure interests	• Recent advancements • Impact on product specification • Impact on product delivery

Figure 10.2 PEST analysis

Strengths	Weaknesses
Issues such as:	*Issues such as:*
• Patents • Favourable access to customer base • Strong brand	• High costs • Lack of protection • Weak brand • Lack of access to customers
Opportunities	**Threats**
Issues such as:	*Issues such as:*
• Identifiable niche market • New technologies • Unique selling point (USP)	• Shift on customer tastes • New competitors • increased regulations

Figure 10.3 SWOT analysis

▶ Profit and loss statement – years two and three summary.

▶ Cashflow statement – year one detail.

▶ Cashflow statement – years two and three summary.

▶ Balance sheet – years one to three.

How to approach putting this information together and how to present it will be covered in detail in the next chapter.

Exit strategy

You should have a clear exit strategy from the outset. It might not seem a priority to establish an exit at the point when you are setting up your company, but it is important for two reasons. Firstly, any financier will be interested to know how their investment might be treated in the years to come. They will be interested to know whether you are starting this venture with the intention of operating the business in 20 years' time or whether you plan to start, build and sell it on in three years. This point is incredibly pertinent for any backer, especially private investors or venture capitalists.

The second point of importance is that some operational decisions may be driven by the desired term of the company. For example, you might be more willing to sign a 10-year lease and pay less overall if you plan to operate the company for a longer period; however if the venture is to provide you with an exit after fewer years, you might be looking for a shorter-term lease and may have to pay a higher rate. This principle applies to many buying decisions and influences how arrangements are set up with distributors, employees, customers and suppliers.

Activity: Compiling your business plan

Write down some ideas for the following components of your business plan:

1. Mission statement

2. Goals and objectives ➤

---

3. Key management team

4. Product detail

5. Environmental analysis.

Just start with these sections for now. Once you have jotted down some ideas for each of these sections, read them through to make sure they have a common theme or message. There must be a logical link from one section to the next; for example, your goals and objectives should address your mission statement; your management team biographies should reflect experience needed to achieve the goals and objectives and be able to deliver the product. Your product detail should also link into your goals and objectives and mission statement. Keep editing the content until each point addresses the other four points sufficiently. The financial detail of the business plan will be covered in chapter 11.

What do I do with my business plan?

Once you have completed the first draft of your business plan, leave it alone for a few days. It is possible to become so smothered by the detail that you may miss either factual or grammatical errors and the business plan must look polished before any third party looks at it. After a few days break, review the entire document for statistical, grammatical and presentational accuracy of content. Check that references link to each other; for example, if your final summary states that profit is £100,000 make sure this is backed up in your financial summary and that any other point of reference tallies with this information.

Once you are satisfied with the content and presentation, give the document to a trusted friend or relative to read. A fresh pair of eyes may see mistakes or query inconsistencies. Not all of us have perfect English or word processing skills, so ask someone who has strengths in areas where you may have a weakness; incorporate any relevant suggestions they may have.

Now that you have a business plan which accurately summarises your product and proposed business activities, it's time to send it out. Identify relevant, useful parties who may be interested in looking at your business plan. The following table identifies some business activity objectives and their relevant parties.

Business activity	Relevant parties
Funding	Banks, private investors, business angels, merchant banks, invoice discounting companies, other financial institutions.
Recruit a team	Targeted employees, distributors.
Source raw materials for production	Suppliers, warehouse, carriage companies.
Business set-up	Landlord, business support companies, insurance companies.

Bear in mind that you would not necessarily show the entire business plan to all of the above parties. Companies would like to see the financial section of your business plan to understand how you intend to pay their bills, especially if you are seeking credit. Be flexible in relation to people's requirements, and try to be as accommodating as possible without giving away too much information. Always ask interested parties to sign a non-disclosure agreement before sending them a copy of your business plan to protect your interests.

Presentation of your business plan

The next step is to identify the list of people and companies to whom you would like to show the business plan as information. Print your business plan in full colour on good quality paper. Give it a cover, featuring the name of the company, the product and your contact details. It is always a good idea to have the business plan bound, including a sheet of card as the last page to keep the document tidy. You can do this yourself or have it done professionally at minimal cost. These small points of presentational detail will make a big difference, as your potential investor may be the fifth person in a company to read your business plan – so make sure it can stand up to a bit of handling. Never send an unsolicited business plan as it will quite often be ignored, or may even end up in the wrong hands. Find out the name, position and address of the recipient of your business plan and send it marked for their attention.

Before sending out your business plan, spend some time practising how you will present its content. Hopefully, within days, you will hear back from one of the recipients and you will be invited to a meeting to present your business concept in further detail. You must be able to present the information in your business plan with confidence and preferably without using your notes as a prompt. You should know your information inside and out and be able to speak about it while providing further information as requested.

Conclusion

It is important to get your business plan right before you launch your company. This isn't easy to achieve as there is unlikely to be actual trading history upon which to base assumptions and claims. Do your best to present clearly how you envisage the company operating and why you feel it will be successful. Ultimately, this document is a sales tool; so while it should be realistic, it should also be written in confident language and assume that the end result will be achieved within the timeframe stated. Use positive language, such as 'will happen', rather than 'may happen' to encourage the reader.

Practise delivering the content of the business plan until you know it inside out and can deliver the essence of the information easily, whether in a two minute phone conversation or a one-hour meeting. This is your time to shine as the owner of your business and give a third party confidence in your Big Idea, your company and in you personally.

11

What do you include in the financial section of the business plan?

As promised in chapter 10, this chapter will explain the financial summary section of your business plan; it will answer the specific question of how and what you will need to finance your business, in order to begin operations and grow your company to meet your goals and objectives.

How will your business make money?

Your product needs to be sufficiently profitable to support your business, so by this stage of the planning process, it's important to ensure that the basic figures add up. This section of the book provides an early reality check that will help you to avoid costly mistakes at a later stage. Lessons learnt now could save you time, money, energy and heartache further down the track. You will need to answer the following three questions about your product:

1. Will enough people want to buy it?
2. What is the retail price?
3. How much will it cost you to deliver?

The combined answers to these three questions will give you an idea of whether or not your Big Idea can be a profitable product for the business. We'll now look at these three points in turn.

Will enough people want to buy it?

You need to establish the demand and supply for your product. Perhaps you feel that 2,500 units will be sold in the first year. Does this tie in with your market assumptions? What percentage of the total market does this figure represent? If 2,500 products are to be in demand, will you have the ability or capacity to produce this number of units? The figure will represent the quantity 'Q' in your financial planning.

What is the retail price?

Establish what you think people will pay for this product. Base this assumption on the pricing of competitor products in the market. Can you charge a premium for a unique selling point (USP)? If your price is over the market odds, you must be able to justify to your customers why they should pay more. For example, if you intend to set a retail price of £75, you must be able to justify the rationale behind it and it must generate sufficient profits to cover your costs. Your sales price is represented by 'P' in your financial summary.

How much will it cost you to deliver?

In order to calculate the total cost of delivery, start by calculating all of the costs that will go in to producing one unit of your product. You should include the cost of the raw materials, labour, carriage and any other costs associated directly with bringing the product to market. These costs are called *direct costs*. They are represented by 'C' in your financial summary. (For the purposes of direct costs, ignore overheads at this point; these are fixed costs, such as rent.)

Use the following formula to calculate the basic profitability of your Big Idea:

Q =	Quantity	2,500
P =	Sales price	£75
C =	Direct costs (costs of sale)	£30

$$\text{Gross profit} = (P\text{-}C) \times Q$$
$$= (£75\text{--}£30) \times 2,500$$
$$= £112,500$$

You will quite often hear the term gross profit. This simply means the profit before any overheads are accounted for. The term gross margin is also used in place of gross profit. Once gross profit has been calculated, make sure it will cover your overheads. Overheads are the sum total of all fixed costs, such as rent.

Business plan – financial summary

Building the financial summary section of your business plan can be a daunting task, especially if you do not have a financial background. At this stage, however, you just need to be comfortable with the basics. As the owner of a small business, you should be conversant with the terms used in this section; so if you are not already comfortable with this area of business, use this section as a learning tool for terminology as well as content and format.

Providing financial information can be challenging because different people, namely investors, will want to see different pieces of information in different formats. In my experience, the following recommended format should meet the general need of those using your business plan, as well as giving you a framework around which to build your financial summary. Complete the information slowly and make sure that every piece of information used has been generated with confidence. If information provided is an assumption, make sure this is made clear to the reader; if it is based on fact provide the reference to the data in an appendix.

The key is to provide this basic financial summary and then build upon it to meet the specific needs of the reader. For example, you may submit a business plan to an investor who understands the content, but who may also require information on user assumptions, or more detail on how the cost of sales has been determined. You cannot possibly hope to answer everyone's questions in the two pages you have available for your financial summary, so use the templates required, which will get you about 80 per cent of the way. The sections of the financial summary section of your business plan are repeated here for ease of reference. (They are also listed in chapter 10):

▶ Product profitability and sales volume assumptions.

▶ Profit and loss statement – year one detail.

▶ Profit and loss statement – years two and three summary.

▶ Cashflow statement – year one detail.

▶ Cashflow statement – years two and three summary.

▶ Balance sheet – years one to three.

Planning horizon

The timeframe covered by your financial summary is known as the planning horizon. You should always present the first twelve months of your business plan in detail. It is sufficient to present the following years in summary. The summary can be extended into a five-year forecast if you think it paints a more accurate picture of the growth and development of the product and business. However, most seasoned investors will look only at the first three years. They know that owners of start-up businesses have to make assumptions, so a planning horizon of any longer than three years is likely to be based on pure conjecture. It is easier and more accurate to keep the planning to three years.

A note on spreadsheets

The easiest way to set up your financial summary is by using Excel or a similar spreadsheet program. You may be surprised to find that some people try to use word processing to present financial information. This just doesn't work. A spreadsheet program will allow for changes to be made to mathematical content and the presentation of data that can then filter through the document, without having to recalculate all the figures manually.

There is no need to buy an expensive modelling program unless you have a particularly sophisticated financial model, which is unlikely at this stage in the life of your company. The advantage of Excel is that it is cheap and easy to use. If you buy yourself an easy 'how-to' guide to make sure you're making the most of the program, it is unlikely you will ever need to use another tool to prepare your financial planning during the life of your company. The next sections look at the financial summary and the format of each in more detail.

Product profitability and sales volume statement

Before setting up a profit and loss statement it is useful to establish the key factors that will contribute to the profitability of the company. Laying out these factors in a separate section allows clarity of thought as well as providing future reference for yourself and those using the business plan. This section should include the following pieces of information:

▶ Retail price per unit of each product type.

▶ Discounts (for example, for distributors, early settlement of account, or sales).

▶ Sales volume per unit of each product type.

▶ Cost of sales per unit of each product type (detailed).

COMPANY NAME
Financial summary
For the period 1 January 2007 to 31 December 2009
Product profitability and sales volume statement

	Jan-07 £	Feb-07 £	Mar-07 £	Apr-07 £	May-07 £	Jun-07 £	Jul-07 £	Aug-07 £	Sep-07 £	Oct-07 £	Nov-07 £	Dec-07 £	2007 £	2008 £	Growth from 2007	2009 £	Growth from 2008
Retail price per unit																	
Product a	X																
Product b																	
Product c																	
Sales volumes																	
Product a	Y																
Product b																	
Product c																	
Turnover (£)																	
Product a	XxY=T																
Product b																	
Product c																	
Total turnover (£)																	
Discounts																	
Product a	U																
Product b																	
Product c																	
Less cost of sales per unit																	
Product a	V																
Product b																	
Product c																	
Gross profit																	
Product a	=T-U-V																
Product b																	
Product c																	
Total gross profit (GP)																	

Figure 11.1 Product profitability and sales volume statement

Every item that makes up the gross profit of each product should be included in the summary. Figure 11.1 is an example of the format for a product profitability and sales volume statement.

1. Start with the revenue of each product. Insert this figure under the heading for each individual product.

2. Enter the sales volumes per month that you expect from each product. You can also break these down by geographical location if it makes analysis simpler.

3. Enter any discounts that you may have to pay for distributors to act as a sales force. They can take anywhere from 10 per cent to around 50 per cent of revenue depending on their influence in a particular market. Discounts for sales offers and early payment settlement should also be included to reduce the revenue generated by the sale of the product.

4. The total discounts are then deducted from the turnover of each product.

5. Enter the cost of sales for each product. You may want to have a separate calculation for this if there are many components for each product.

6. Deduct the cost of sales from the turnover total to calculate the gross profit (gross profit equals retail price per unit x sales volume less discounts less cost of sales).

7. The gross profit figure is the contribution towards to your overhead base.

Compiling a level of detail at this stage will stand you in good stead for the future as it will be easier to look back and see how certain figures were calculated. It will also provide a level of transparency for external parties who will be interested in determining how the gross profit is reached. The information is useful for future analysis too, such as comparing the profitability of products. Once you are satisfied that the product profitability report indicates the correct gross profit, you can start to set up the profit and loss statement.

COMPANY NAME
Financial summary
For the period 1 January 2007 to 31 December 2009

Profit and loss statement

	Jan-07 £	Feb-07 £	Mar-07 £	Apr-07 £	May-07 £	Jun-07 £	Jul-07 £	Aug-07 £	Sep-07 £	Oct-07 £	Nov-07 £	Dec-07 £	2007 £	2008 £	Growth from 2007	2009 £	Growth from 2008
Sales turnover	A																
less cost of sales	B																
Gross profit (GP)	A−B=C																
GP%																	
Overheads																	
Administration staff costs																	
Property costs																	
Postage, phone & fax																	
Administration and office costs																	
Advertising and marketing																	
Travel and business entertainment																	
Finance costs																	
Professional fees																	
Other costs																	
Total overheads	D																
Earnings before interest & tax (EBIT)	C−D=E																
EBIT %of sales turnover																	
Interest paid	F																
Interest received	G																
Earnings before tax (EBT)	E−F+G=H																
Corporation tax	I																
Profits after tax	H−I																

Figure 11.2 Profit and loss statement

Profit and loss statement (P&L)

The profit and loss statement is a summary of the revenues and costs of the business, which provides a picture of the profits over a certain period. Any item that impacts on the profitability of a business should be included in the profit and loss statement. Construction of the profit and loss statement is aided by use of a template, such as the example provided in Figure 11.2. Every business is different and yet statutory reporting requirements are the same for all private companies in the UK and therefore, it makes sense to use a generic format to start with and expand specific areas to better reflect your individual business.

The profit and loss statement should be kept simple. Add a relevant account or additional detail where required; but try to maintain the overall format to accommodate any changes. The table below highlights the main profit and loss items on the statement and their purpose.

Main heading	Sub-heading	Purpose of account
Turnover	Sales income	Revenue generated from the retail price of the product.
Cost of sales	Raw materials	Every component or item that is considered a direct cost of the business should be treated as a cost of sale; that is, any item that is directly apportioned to creating the product and preparing it for sale.
Cost of sales	Marketing and distribution	The cost of delivering the product to market.
Cost of sales	Customer discounts	Any discount given to retail, wholesale outlets or distributors that is deducted from the retail price.
Gross profit		Turnover less cost of sales (calculation).
Overheads	Salaries	Classify salaries between permanent, temporary, contractors and so on. Each different type of labour used should be reported separately.

Main heading	Sub-heading	Purpose of account
Overheads	Rent and premises	Include rent, rates, utilities and other costs associated with maintaining the property and relevant to the operations of the business.
Overheads	Office expenses	Other fixed expenses relating to the running of the office and the business infrastructure.
EBITDA	Earnings Before Interest, Tax, Depreciation and Amortisation	Gross profit less overheads (calculation).
Other	Interest	Interest payable on debt or other interest liabilities should be included.
Other	Tax	Corporation tax liability as calculated on pre-tax profits.
Other	Depreciation and amortisation	Fixed assets suffer depreciation and intangible assets (such as goodwill) suffer amortisation.
Profits after tax		EBITDA less interest, tax, depreciation and amortisation (calculation). These are distributable profits and may be taken as dividends or carried into the next period as retained earnings.

Balance sheet

The balance sheet is simply a snapshot of the company assets and liabilities at any point in time. It is most commonly calculated at the end of each month and at the end of the financial year. It is common practice to present the balance sheet along with the profit and loss statement and the cashflow; together they are the three primary financial statements. Investors will use the balance sheet to assess the level of assets, liabilities and equity that shareholders have in the company and how this is likely to change over the planning horizon, as a result of the planned trading of the business.

Use figure 11.3 as a template to prepare your balance sheet information. You need only present a balance sheet figure at the end of each of the first three years in your business plan; there is no need to provide a monthly balance sheet. Again, it is important to understand the main headings of the balance sheet, but it is not

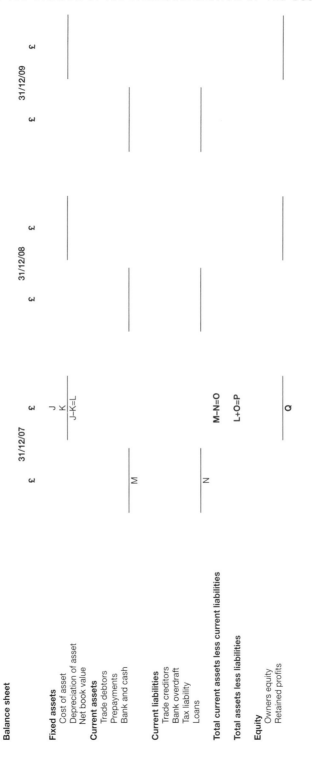

COMPANY NAME
Financial summary
For the period 1 January 2007 to 31 December 2009

Balance sheet

	31/12/07	£	31/12/08	£	31/12/09	£
	£		£		£	
Fixed assets						
Cost of asset	J					
Depreciation of asset	K					
Net book value	J–K=L					
Current assets						
Trade debtors						
Prepayments						
Bank and cash	M					
Current liabilities						
Trade creditors						
Bank overdraft						
Tax liability						
Loans	N					
Total current assets less current liabilities	M–N=O					
Total assets less liabilities	L+O=P					
Equity						
Owners equity						
Retained profits	Q					

check 0   *P should equal Q*

Figure 11.3 Balance sheet

115

important for the owner of a small business to understand the
workings behind the financial standards that drive the accounts –
that can be left to your accountant. The main headings on the
balance sheet that you need to understand are as follows. While
there are many more accounts on the balance sheet than those
listed, these are the common accounts that a start-up business will
display on its starting balance sheet.

Main heading	Sub-heading	Purpose of account
Fixed asset	Asset – cost	The invoice value of the asset (excluding VAT). This figure should be the net amount that the business actually paid for the asset.
Fixed asset	Asset – depreciation	The depreciation of the asset is the value that is taken to the profit and loss statement as a cost of operating the business. Assets should be given a 'useful economic life' over which period the asset is usually fully depreciated.
Fixed asset	Net book value (NBV) of asset	The cost of an asset less its depreciation (calculation).
Current asset	Trade debtors	The value of money owed by customers to the business for goods sold on credit.
Current asset	Prepayments and deposits	Payments made as deposits and held on account by a third party; prepayments for goods or services that will be used in future periods.
Current asset	Bank account and cash	Total of bank accounts and any cash held on hand, such as petty cash.
Current liability	Trade creditors	The value of money owed to suppliers by the business for goods purchased on credit.
Current liability	Bank overdraft	Money owed to a lender in the form of an overdraft or other short-term loan facility.
Current liability	Tax liability	Corporation tax liability based on profits, PAYE tax for employees and National Insurance contributions owed to Inland Revenue.
Current liability	Loans	Any other third-party loans (due within 12 months).
Long-term liability	Loans	Any loan (due in periods greater than 12 months from balance sheet date).
Equity	Owners equity brought forward	Total value of assets less liabilities brought forward from the previous reporting period.
Equity	Retained profits	Total profits generated and retained by the business for use in future periods.

Remember that your balance sheet should always balance, as the following equation sets out:

Total assets – Total liabilities = Total equity

A positive equity balance means that the assets are greater than the liabilities, whereas a negative equity balance indicates that liabilities are greater than assets. A negative equity balance should be explained with a brief statement, with an indication of when a positive balance might be achieved by the business.

Cashflow statement

Many potential investors will flick through the product and market sections of your business plan and then go straight to the cashflow statement. It can be argued that the cashflow statement is the most important report a small business owner will produce and maintain in the first 12 months of his business, as liquidity and cash are critical to the survival of a small business.

There is a separate section later in this chapter entitled 'cash is king' which further explains the importance of cash, its control and effective management. It is important that you view cash management and reporting as a priority once you launch your business; an investor may even require weekly reports to ensure the business (and his investment) is being managed effectively. Be prepared to become intimate with the cashflow of your business as, without effective control over this all important asset, you may not have a business to operate. For now, let's look at the format of the cashflow statement and how it fits into the financial summary section of the business plan. (See figure 11.4.)

The cashflow statement is a record of the cash inflows and outflows of the business during a fixed period. It is easiest to think of it as the actual movement of cash. Do not make the common mistake of confusing cash with profits. This concept is addressed in further detail later in the chapter.

COMPANY NAME
Financial summary
For the period 1 January 2007 to 31 December 2009

Cashflow statement

	Jan-07 £	Feb-07 £	Mar-07 £	Apr-07 £	May-07 £	Jun-07 £	Jul-07 £	Aug-07 £	Sep-07 £	Oct-07 £	Nov-07 £	Dec-07 £	2007 £	*Growth from 2007* 2008 £	*Growth from 2008* 2009 £
Cash inflows															
Cash sales															
Credit sales															
Sale of assets															
Interest received															
Other cash inflows															
Total cash inflows	R														
Cash outflows															
Cost of sales															
Overheads:															
Administration staff costs															
Property costs															
Postage, phone & fax															
Administration and office costs															
Advertising and marketing															
Travel and business entertainment															
Finance costs															
Professional fees															
Other costs															
Puchase of fixed assets															
Interest payable															
Other cash outflows															
Total cash outflows	S														

Cash balance brought forward	U
Total net cash inflow (outflow) in the period	R–S=T
Cash balance carried forward	U–T

Figure 11.4 Cashflow statement

It is worth taking some time to understand the distinction between cash and profits as this is often an area of confusion among business managers. The cashflow statement simply adds together all of the cash inflows and then deducts the cash outflows to produce a cash balance. Do not try to overcomplicate the cashflow statement as it needs to be kept simple.

Cash inflows might include:

▶ Sales receipts – do not include sales made on credit until the period in which they will actually be received and take discounts given into consideration

▶ Sale of assets

▶ Interest receivable

Cash outflows might include:

▶ Cost of sale expenditure

▶ Overheads

▶ Interest payable

▶ Purchase of fixed assets

The construction of the cashflow statement is quite simple in that it is generally a replication of the profit and loss format, taking into consideration the timing of cash inflows and outflows. The process of creating a cashflow statement is as follows. (Remember to focus on reflecting the cashflows *in the period in which they are to be received or paid by the business*.)

1. Start with the profit and loss statement items.
2. Make the necessary adjustments for timing differences. For example, if sales are to be received in the following month, reflect June sales in the July cashflow.
3. Remove items from the profit and loss statement that do not represent a cash movement, such as depreciation.
4. Add to the cashflow balance sheet items that will impact on cash inflows and outflows in the period, such as purchase or sale of fixed assets.

5. Add a line for the opening cash balance to be brought forward.

6. Add a line for the closing balance to be carried forward.

7. Make sure it all adds up.

The cashflow total will not balance with your profit and loss statement. There are items, such as depreciation, that do not require cash movement and timing differences and which may see a cash item reflected in a different period from the profit or loss. The closing balance line will indicate a positive cash balance (surplus) or a negative cash balance (deficit). Any indications of a deficit should be explained as these are periods where financing may be required. The outcome of the cashflow statement will provide you with the information you need regarding how much working capital (cash or financing) you will need to start and operate your business. We will look at different financing options in chapter 12.

Cashflow planning horizon

Prepare a monthly cashflow for the first 12 months and then an annual summary for the second and third years. From an operational point of view it is advisable to maintain a weekly cashflow report for the first six months or until such time as you better understand your business and its cash requirements. This will be covered in more detail in section seven.

A note on VAT in the cashflow statement

The cashflow should include both input and output VAT. Remember that the cashflow statement is only concerned with amounts of cash coming in and going out of the business. As VAT is both paid and received by the business it should be included in all cashflow calculations. Make sure your sales and any relevant expenses are inclusive of VAT in the cashflow statement. You must also include the timings of when VAT payments or receipts from Inland Revenue are expected to impact on the business.

Cash is king

Cash is without question the most important resource in your business. Your treatment of cash from Big Idea development through to operating and selling your company can be the difference between success and failure and you rarely get a second chance to right wrongs. One of the outcomes of your business plan is the cashflow statement, which will indicate how much cash you will need to start up and run your business. There are a few important points to remember about cash as the following sections explain.

Working capital management

Cashflow can be improved through effective working capital management. The techniques following are common methods of using working capital efficiently.

▶ Reduce stocks as high stock levels can be an expensive luxury for a lean business. They tie up capital and add to the cost of stockholding.

▶ Effective credit control to reduce debtors.

▶ Adopting longer credit terms with supplier.

Profits do not equal cash

Cash is all about cash inflows and outflows. When focusing on your liquidity, forget about accounting issues such as accruals and profits, just consider the cash that is actually coming in and going out. In addition, don't forget about discounts that may have been promised, which your customers can deduct from their payment.

Some of the key reasons for profits not equalling cash include:

▶ Debtor and credit repayment agreements

▶ Stock purchases and lead time

▶ Accruals and prepayments

▶ Depreciation of fixed assets

Assess how closely your P&L relates to the actual cash movement in your business. If it's largely a cash business with fast moving stock then you will probably find that your P&L is a good reflection of cashflow; however once the above mentioned items start to creep in, you could see the two statements diverge. Even if you are making profits, if you don't have the cash to pay debts as and when they fall due, your company could be put into liquidation or have some operational constraints put on it by a creditor. As a new business, keep focused on your cashflow.

Credit control

Companies approach the issue of credit control in different ways. Your approach will depend largely on your relationship with your customers, how many there are, and the amounts and terms of their credit – especially in relation to your turnover. The higher the exposure the more attention they should receive from the person controlling cash in your business. Different approaches to credit control will work in different situations: developing a relationship, writing letters and even adopting a stern voice can work wonders – or not; which is why it's important to tailor credit control to the specific needs of your business and your customer.

Cash deficit

If you are looking at a cash deficit in your forecast, take immediate steps to ensure it doesn't impact adversely on operations. This may mean a call to the bank manager to discuss a short-term overdraft, extending terms with suppliers, or calling upon directors for loans. Focus on the core business through difficult cash-poor times as this is no time for non-essential spending.

Contingency

There will always be a cash expense item that pops up at a time when the company is running on limited cashflow. The best forecasts cannot plan for every eventuality, so it is essential to have some form of contingency planning in place. I generally allow for 2 per cent of turnover per month as cash contingency. Build this in to your forecast.

Help with the financial statements

The sections above should give you an understanding of what information is required to produce basic financial statements for the business plan. Any business owner should be able to understand these fundamentals. However, if you do not feel confident with the information you have put together, seek professional help. Sometimes, it can be wise to seek initial advice from an accountant or business professional who has experience with financial reporting. A little advice early on could save you time and money further down the track.

Conclusion

Preparing the financial summary section of your business plan can be a daunting task. Keep it simple. You don't need to be an accountant to get your basic maths and assumptions right. Follow the simple steps provided in this chapter and you will have the tools to generate sufficiently detailed financial planning for your business plan.

If you are still unsure as to the integrity of your financial summary, it is worth asking someone with experience in these matters to take a look at it, rather than rely on the data or submit it to an investor with incorrect information. Investors will raise questions about your entire venture if the numbers don't stack up, so it really is important they are well thought out, correctly presented and can be substantiated with factual data. Remember – cash is king and cash does not necessarily equal profits. As long as you forecast and keep a firm eye on what your cashflow is doing, you will be one step ahead of the game.

Now that you have created your business plan and are sure about the level of finance required for your business, it's time to think about how to make it work as a business operation. You will need a framework for a company, and a team; so we will look at these in the next two sections, starting with your team.

12

How should you finance the business?

There will come a time during the transition from Big Idea to operating a business when you will need to think about how you are going to finance the process. Start-ups often need finance early in the process, but it is possible to go a long way down the set-up path without needing any substantial capital. You need to establish when the need to finance the business will happen and how much cash you will need. This information is the output from the cashflow statement that was covered in the previous chapter and should always be included in your business plan. There are two phases of finance to consider for the business: seed capital and operating capital.

Seed capital

The money (or assets) required to get the idea off the ground is known as seed capital. It may be needed for a sample run of your product, for initial marketing or for the hire of premises. This expenditure will cover the set-up phase of your business.

Operating capital

Once you have set up your business, you may need to have some operating capital to cover expenditure until such point as revenues can generate a profit and subsequent cash surplus. The term of this cash (or asset) requirement will depend on your business and its success in the market.

Equity vs. loan

There are two main approaches to raising either seed or operating capital. Firstly, a financier can provide cash or business assets in exchange for a shareholding (equity) in your company. Generally this will be a percentage of ordinary shares based on an agreed valuation of the business. A shareholding will generally bring with it some element of control or management input from the financier or his delegate, such as a board seat (statutory director). Second, a loan is provided to the business by a lender, as an amount of cash or an asset, with an agreement that the business will repay the capital with an interest premium. A business loan can take many forms and can be flexible depending on the needs and financial position of the business.

Start-up companies often prefer a loan option for operational seed capital rather than equity as the valuation of an early stage company is likely to be low: quite often much lower than the business owner would care to admit. This is despite the fact that loan finance often costs the business more in terms of cash than issuing equity. The risk for an investor is much higher with a start-up and so the reward is generally required to be high, reflecting the level of risk and financial exposure.

Sources of capital

There are five main sources of capital that are available to the owner of a small business start-up:

▶ Banks

- Friends and family
- Private investors
- Government grants
- Own cash reserves

Banks

Many banks will offer business loans to start-up companies that they perceive as relatively low risk and where there are assets against which a loan can be secured. If there are insufficient assets, the bank will expect the directors to provide a personal guarantee against the value of the loan, using their personal assets. Banks will also provide other forms of credit including overdrafts, which can be a useful bridging tool; however, overdrafts can be an expensive source of finance. It is very rare that banks will require (or want) equity in a company.

Friends and family

Friends and family may be in a position to offer a loan or their expertise for your new venture. If you decide to take up this option, treat the transaction with the same professionalism that you would any other. This means you should reach an agreement with the lender under normal commercial terms, applying the market interest rates and repayment terms. It is also wise to ensure that the lender has read your business plan and understands the risks as well as the opportunities that this investment will offer them. In short, treat family and friends as you would any other investor. This approach will help to iron out any potential disputes should they arise in the future. Another point to consider is that, should the venture not be as successful as originally planned, you may put a personal relationship at risk as well as a business arrangement. Weigh up carefully what may be lost as well as what can be gained from borrowing from a friend or family member.

Private investors

There are an increasing number of private investors who will invest in start-up companies. As the investment risk is perceived as high at this stage of development, an investor will require a higher level of return than when investing in an established company. Private investors can often cut through the red tape that surrounds many larger institutions when looking at investment in a start-up. Financial institutions must consider the impact of the level of exposure on their own shareholders, so they often approach investment in start-ups with caution. Private investors – also referred to as 'business angels' – are generally found through word of mouth. If this is the path you wish to take, start spreading the word via members of the business community, including those in professions such as law, accounting and commerce; tell them that you wish to meet potential private investors for your venture.

Government grants

The UK government actively promotes small business; new business start-ups provide taxable revenue and help to reduce the employment rate. Encouragement for small companies is generated by the provision of financial support and information-based support via government grants and initiatives. The Department of Trade and Industry is the best source of information about government support and will provide advice based on your business requirements. Make sure you read the fine print of any agreement and that you meet the initial and ongoing terms and criteria as stated.

Own cash reserves

The cheapest way of starting up and supporting a new business is often by using your own resources. The only exception to this would be if you are currently earning a very high return on an investment, which outweighs the cost of capital from business borrowing from another source. Make sure that you account accurately for every penny that you invest in your company in order to report the full amount of your investment.

Cost of capital

Whichever source of finance you choose, make sure you are aware of the full cost of using the facility. This is called the cost of capital. You will be given an interest rate and repayment terms and often charged an arrangement fee. Read all of the small print and weigh all of your options up carefully. If you use two different sources of finance, ensure they can be used together; provide full disclosure of all of your borrowings to each party. Keep a note of the cost of capital as this will need to be factored into your financial projections.

Conclusion

Working captital is essential for all businesses at some stage if they are to expand and grow. Tread carefully when making decisions on borrowing and take your time to weigh up the risks and benefits of each proposal as these financial relationships could last for the life of your business.

13

CHAPTER THIRTEEN
What are the common pitfalls of business?

Most people have either a positive or a negative outlook on life – their glass may be half full or half empty. Being able to approach financial and business planning in a positive manner is a great entrepreneurial quality, though there comes a time when realism (or pessimism) has a role to play too. My former colleagues used to refer to me as a 'wet blanket' as I would remind them of what could go wrong if things were insufficiently planned or researched.

Common pitfalls for a new business

It's easy to disregard the oncoming hurricane if the business is sailing along on calm seas. Always beware of pitfalls. Learn from those who have come before you and be aware of some of the common issues that new businesses face:

▶ Running out of cash
▶ Not knowing your market
▶ People problems
▶ Supply
▶ Demand
▶ Ego

Running out of cash

Cash is king. Keep an eye on how much cash you have and how much cash you need – now and for the next 12 months at least. Your cash forecast should not be neglected, especially when you are starting out. It should be the first and last document you look at each day.

Not knowing your market

You have a Big Idea, but don't think for a second that there aren't other Big Ideas being created, developed and worked into operating companies every day. Know your enemy. You should have an intimate knowledge of the competition and an awareness of new products and innovations that may impact on your business. Monitor the industry for new entrants as well as existing competitors with new products; similarly, ensure you are at the forefront of your customers' minds and that you can adapt as their needs change. Use people who know your market best to provide you with this data and research, which will save you time and money. Innovation and continuing product development are integral to the success and ongoing strategy of any small business that engenders creativity and wants to satisfy customer requirements.

People problems

An experienced managing director of a high-profile company once told me that if he could operate his company without relying on people it would take away 80 per cent of his headaches. Inevitably, people are self-serving. They are motivated by what will improve their life and working environment, which isn't always in line with the needs of the company. Make sure that everyone throughout the business shares the same business goals. If you can align these goals your people problems should significantly reduce. This logic applies to customers, suppliers and other stakeholders too (where possible), not just employees.

Some years ago, I was parachuted into a struggling company that had a large sales force who were remunerated on units sold only. It transpired that they were selling the goods for less than cost price so that they could register a sale; this practice carried on for over a year before it was identified as a reason why the company was losing money. The sales team's goals were not congruent with the rest of the company's goals. The solution was to change the arrangement so that, if the salesmen sold more units at a better margin, they would benefit along with the company – a successful application of goal congruence.

Supply

To provide a product to customers, you need to ensure that your suppliers supply exactly what you order, when you require it. It helps to establish a working relationship with a small number of suppliers if possible. The early days of your company will be a testing time and there will be a lot of learning on the job. The timely supply of good quality products will smooth the initial months of trading.

Once established, a good continuing relationship with your suppliers will help business, but you will need to keep on top of orders and monitor the delivery of goods accordingly. Even proven suppliers can make mistakes if communication breaks down, so don't be afraid to check on the progress of an order regularly to ensure that it will be delivered on time. Your customers don't care why there is a supply problem, only whether they can buy the product or not. If not, they will generally go elsewhere, rather than wait around for their demand to be met.

Demand

It can be difficult to forecast demand for your product, especially if the product is new to the market. Take-up of a new product is relatively low generally, though there are exceptions to this rule that see new products fly off the shelves. Good planning and market research will allow your business to fulfil customer demand, allowing a margin for increased demand where required. This is nearly impossible to achieve perfectly in year one, though this area of business operations can save you a lot of money when you get it right. Many businesses have fallen due to holding onto too much or too little stock, so investigate the stockholding systems available to you (such as those running a 'just in time' or 'first in–first out' policy) and apply the best methodology for your business.

Ego

Ego as a reason for business failure could fill a book in itself. Listen to the people around you! Many business failures can be related either directly or indirectly to a decision that was made out of arrogance or vanity and without the proper consultative process. I've seen this happen too many times. Many problems can be avoided if the main decision-maker is able to admit that they are wrong or don't know all there is to know about business.

Conclusion

If an entrepreneur monitors the above issues within their business, success will be much more likely. It isn't easy to keep juggling every aspect of your business, but as the owner, that's what you must be able to do. After a while, a lot of what is required will become second nature, though there will always be challenges that will threaten to disrupt the business. The approach you choose to resolve these challenges can mean the difference between success and failure.

4

Key points to remember

Creating a business plan provides clarity of purpose and process for you and third parties who are interested in your venture. The key sections of your business plan are:

- ▶ Mission statement
- ▶ Goals and objectives
- ▶ Key management team
- ▶ Product
- ▶ Environmental analysis
- ▶ Financial summary
- ▶ Exit strategy

Use SWOT and PEST management techniques for environmental analysis.

Learn to present your business plan in front of other parties. You must know all of the information about your business and understand enough to answer any likely questions. Practise your presentation of the facts as it could be the difference between success and failure.

Identify sales quantity, sales prices and expenses to determine how the company will make money.

The financial summary section of your business plan should include the following sections:

- ▶ Product profitability and sales volume statement

- Profit and loss statement
- Balance sheet
- Cashflow statement

Seed and operating capital are methods of financing the business which can be gained from a wide range of parties, these include:

- Banks
- Family and friends
- Private investors
- Government grants
- Own cash reserves

Remember to calculate the cost of capital of whichever source of capital you choose.

Beware the common pitfalls of business:

- Running out of cash
- Not knowing your market
- People problems
- Supply
- Demand
- Ego

5

Team

You have taken time to consider your Big Idea, develop a product, create a marketing strategy and compile a business plan. Now it's time to think about what kind of support you need to deliver your product and run your business: who do you want or need to help you out? Don't think you have to do it all alone. Even if you think you want to, you will probably change your mind once you have started your company. Start thinking about who you need in your internal and external team now.

Chapter 14 – Who should you hire to help?

While you are likely to want to keep costs low, it is probable that you will need some help in the early stages of your business. Many new business owners underestimate just how time consuming some tasks – both core and subsidiary – can be. However, hiring the right person can be a challenge – especially for a new business. The person that you select may not have sufficient confidence in the business and you may need to convince your potential employee about your concept and strategy. Hiring for a start-up can be more complex that hiring for an established company, so you should have an awareness of some interview and management techniques before you start.

Chapter 15 – What external resources are available to help?

Not all help has to be employed labour. There are many external resources available to a new business. These can often be a cost-effective way of obtaining much needed help in areas of your business such as administration, marketing, sales and operations. Be aware of the resources that are available to you, starting with those that are around you.

CHAPTER FOURTEEN
Who should you hire to help?

Hiring a team for your new venture can be difficult. You need to find people who will buy into your Big Idea as much as you do. A person joining a start-up will need to take a leap of faith in you as the business owner and vice versa, in that you are sharing part of a special experience with someone who may or may not be new to you. Keep your personal and business requirements firmly in mind and apply the simple techniques outlined in this chapter to ensure you hire the right person for your company.

Can I do it on my own?

The answer to this question is generally no; and you don't have to. You will need either internal or external resources to aid you in your journey to set up your own business. The key is to be able to identify your team requirements and establish how best to find the people that you need. The focus of this chapter is on creating an internal team. External resources are considered in chapter 15.

When considering who you need as part of your internal team, you will first need to weigh up a number of considerations:

▶ Do I have skills that are best performed solo or as part of a team?

▶ Am I better off teaming up with someone with complementary skills?

- ▶ Who can I afford?
- ▶ Which areas of business are my strongest and weakest points?
- ▶ What are the market expectations for my skills? Am I as marketable as I think I am?
- ▶ What is my maximum capacity?

Let's start with the final point as it's often the most difficult to quantify and it can be difficult to admit when you are overstretched, especially when you are operating as your own boss.

How do I know when I've reached maximum capacity?

You may be unaware when you are reaching maximum capacity and it is often the case that the owners of small businesses work longer hours that their salaried counterparts. Don't allow yourself to become so overstretched that the quality of your work suffers. It would be better to hire someone to help before you reach this point, rather than trying to struggle to do everything yourself.

A common complaint amongst small business owners is that too much time is spent on administration and compliance issues and there is not enough time to focus on the core business – whether development, sales, design or another function deemed to be central to the operations of the business. You know that you have reached maximum capacity when the core requirements of the business are not being met.

Should I work with my partner?

Working with your wife, husband, girlfriend, boyfriend or even a good friend can be a very rewarding experience – or it can be a recipe for disaster. Regardless of the quality of your personal relationship with your partner, it is important that you approach the business side of your relationship with the same level of professionalism that you would apply to working with a complete stranger.

I have worked with many husband and wife teams – some very successful, others not so. The following tips will help you if you intend to rely on an important personal relationship in your business venture:

▶ Set clear lines of job responsibility. Make it clear who is expected to do what and when. This will help you to avoid stepping on each others' toes.

▶ Conduct a progress review every month in the form of a management meeting. Even if there are only two of you, it is important to have a structured meeting where all parties are encouraged to air their views and opinions on certain matters in the operations and management of the company. Unless there is structure you can become so busy performing daily tasks, that you don't take a step back and ask how everything is going overall.

▶ Communicate. If there is a problem, tell your partner in a professional and well thought out manner.

▶ Keep your work and private life separate. While it may be difficult, try to have a rule whereby you discuss business issues in the office and set them aside (as much as possible) when you leave at the end of the day. Similarly, leave pet names for each other at home as use of these can make other employees feel uncomfortable.

▶ Respect each other's views and opinions. Don't underestimate what your partner is capable of. Just because they have never displayed a certain characteristic or skill set in their private life, it doesn't mean they won't shine in a business environment.

While working with a person from your personal life can be a gamble, it can also be a great source of help in your new venture. Follow the rules above and don't take each other for granted to make the relationship work in both a social and business setting.

How do I hire the right person?

Hiring the right person for your small business can be the difference between making life easier and creating a difficult situation. Hiring staff needn't be a complicated process, provided you stick to the basics:

- ▶ Establish which functions the company needs in order to operate effectively and meet projected targets.
- ▶ Identify the skills gaps in each function that you cannot fill yourself, due to insufficient skills and/or time.
- ▶ Calculate your budget for staff. How much can you afford for each identified position?
- ▶ Research job advertisements or talk to recruitment agencies to establish a realistic annual, daily or hourly rate for your resource requirements.
- ▶ Advertise the position in relevant newspapers or local press, or use a recruitment agent.
- ▶ Prepare for the interview by compiling a list of business and personal questions that are important to you and your business (see list below).
- ▶ Carry out the interviews in your place of work (if possible).
- ▶ Hire the right person based on information from the interviews, their experience as per their CV, and your gut feel about the individual as a person.

Interviewing potential employees

Conducting an interview can be daunting if you don't have much experience in this area. It is important to get the most information you can from a potential candidate during the relatively short space of time (around an hour) that you will spend with them. The following list of interview questions may help as a guide to extract important information from the interviewee.

▶ What do you know about the industry?

▶ What is your experience relevant to this job/industry/product?

▶ What duties are you expecting this job to entail?

▶ What are you seeking from this job?

▶ What do you feel you will contribute to the company?

▶ How would your former colleagues/boss describe you?

▶ How do you feel about working for a start-up/small company?

▶ What do you think you'll miss about working for a more established company?

▶ What are your career advancement plans over the next five years and what role do you see this company playing in that advancement?

▶ If offered this job, what factors are important to you when deciding whether to accept or decline the offer?

There are, of course, many other possible interview questions. Try to tailor your questions to the information that is important to you and relevant to your product and the market in which you intend to operate.

We hear a lot about 'corporate culture'. It is important for large multinational companies to get this right; and it is even more important for small companies to hire people who will fit the way the business operates. Ask yourself what kind of business environment you are creating. Is it likely to be lively, spontaneous and active or a more structured and results driven culture? It is often said that an interviewer will make up their mind about an applicant in the first three seconds of an interview. Hire a person who has the experience you require, but more importantly, make sure you hire the person who will fit into the type of environment (culture) that you expect for your business.

Activity: Your ideal employee

Imagine you wish to employ someone to help you start up or operate your new company. Think about what is important to you and your company and also what might be important to a potential employee.

Using the sample interview questions in the section above, write down ten questions that you feel any potential employee must answer to gain a position with you. These will vary from company to company and will often be based on your personal experience of working with people, as well as the position for which you are recruiting. It's important to use the sample questions as a guide and really think about what is relevant to you and your company.

Now that you have your ten questions, provide what is, in your opinion, a perfect answer to each of these questions. Not everyone will have the same view, but it is important to identify your own expectations at this stage.

From your 'perfect' answers to the top ten questions, you should be able to form a picture of your ideal employee. Use this as a foundation upon which to build your team.

Who do I need as part of my team?

The main areas of responsibility to be covered by your team will include:

▶ Product development

- ▶ Sales and after-sales support
- ▶ Marketing
- ▶ Operations and logistics
- ▶ Administration
- ▶ Finance

Each of these areas is important in the set-up and launch of a new business as well as in the continuing operations of a successful company. The key is to understand the importance of each of these roles and the balance between them required in your specific company. Let's look at each of these points in turn:

Product development

Your product is your starting point for the launch of your company and it is the core of the operations and subsequent profits. Whatever else you do in your company, make sure the product works and that it is available in sufficient quantities to meet demand as and when it arises. Continue to focus on product development even after launch to ensure your product is as good and relevant to the market as it was during the start-up phase.

Sales

We are all salesmen. Regardless of your job, you should always be thinking about sales and how to maximise the demand for your product. Selling can be a tiring task and can quite often take up a lot of time without delivering the desired results. Sales staff need to have a positive attitude, a good knowledge of the product and the market; the ability to close a deal, and above all a determination to seek out potential new customers wherever there is an opportunity.

After-sales support

While making the sale is important, so too is keeping the customer you have fought so hard to win. This task can often be time-consuming and thankless, but it is essential to forward growth. It is an important function to fill as it will tell the business owner what is and isn't working about the product or the way it is being delivered. Take the time to understand the feedback you are given and incorporate it into the future workings of the company.

Marketing

Keep up-to-date with the competition and market demands for your product type. It is important to ensure that your knowledge of the environment in which you intend to operate is current and accurate. Customers can be fickle and their tastes can change overnight, so an independent marketing advisor is essential for keeping up with the latest information. You will also need to make the most of your marketing budget – no matter how big or small it is. Try to create opportunities to appear in the press, by giving interviews, creating advertorials, or looking out for marketing opportunities that may arise that will convey your message to the customer.

Operations and logistics

Once you have marketed your product and are making sales, you need to fulfil sales orders. This is carried out via operations and logistics. This role is critical to making sure your customers get exactly what they ordered on time and in good order. The fulfilment process is often fraught with problems that may arise such as goods going missing, destroyed packaging, late deliveries, mislabelling – the list can go on. It is important to keep your operations and logistics process tightly controlled and error free, which often requires a practical focus from an organised mind.

Administration

Don't underestimate the level of administration that is required when you set up a business. You will have internal administration, such as keeping track of the operational cycle between buying and selling, as well as general office requirements. The devil is in the detail when keeping a company running smoothly and often the unsung heroes of a company are the administrative support teams. If you have been employed by a big company where you were supported by an administrative team, you may be in for a shock when you find out how time consuming this type of work can be. The key to success is to be organised and to do things as and when they arise. Don't put anything off until tomorrow as it will generally be more difficult and more expensive to fix.

Finance

A cost/benefit analysis may suggest a strong argument for having someone on board who is thinking about the financial strength of your business and helping you plan as you go. If you have financial training or experience yourself, then this may not be necessary; but if you don't, the benefits of an accounting resource on board cannot be underestimated. The amount of financial support is contingent on what you, as owner/manager know about the size and the complexity of the business. Most start-ups and small- to medium-sized enterprises (SMEs) require a part-time bookkeeper and an experienced, more senior accountant to keep an eye on things once a month. You will soon work out what is needed for you and your company.

What happens if it doesn't work out with your new staff?

All being well, hopefully you won't need to start firing new appointments within the start-up phase of your company. However, it quickly becomes obvious if a member of staff is not right for your business. Perhaps the fit within the corporate culture isn't right, perhaps the employee has misrepresented their abilities, or maybe the company hasn't lived up to their expectations. Whatever the reason, it can be difficult to fire an employee if you do not have a very good reason for doing so, although it is easier while they are working within their probation period; so try to make up your mind about them within that period of time and encourage them to do likewise, as happiness at work is a mutual consideration.

Conclusion

In small companies many, if not all, of the above functions can be fulfilled by a small number of key individuals. The ideal team to have on board when you start up a company will cover the wide range of skills required in any company – whether large or small. You will soon realise the needs of your company, but it's important to realise the benefits that solid human resources and support can bring to a business.

15

What external resources are available to help?

Small businesses are generally on a tight budget and may need to source help that does not come in the form of a salaried employee. There are plenty of external parties who can aid your small business: for a minimal fee, because it's a mutually beneficial relationship, or just because that's their job (for example, government departments). The road to becoming a successful entrepreneur needn't be a lonely one. There are people, agencies and businesses that will each have a direct relationship with your business. These parties are called stakeholders. It is worth knowing who they are and how you can maximise the potential of your relationship with them.

Banks

The relationship you have with your bank will be important in terms of the set-up and operational phase of your business. Once the bank has bought into your Big Idea, your business plan and your operational planning, they may offer to extend you some working capital. Your bank will want your business to succeed so that you can continue to make the interest and capital repayments, so they are often interested in aiding your business proactively. Keep an eye out for new business incentives, such as the offer of two years' free banking; these are quite common and can really benefit a new business as bank fees can add up very quickly. Investigate what other benefits and incentives your bank offers to small businesses.

Competitors

Always keep up-to-date with what your competitors are doing in terms of their trading activity, the products they offer, the way they are marketing their products and whom they are targeting. A wealth of information can be gained from analysing competitor behaviour to see where they have succeeded and failed. Solid data can be difficult to come by as competitors will always want to maintain an advantage if possible. There is, however, plenty of competitor information available on public record at Companies House and the Department of Trade and Industry as well as via industry magazines, trade shows and word of mouth.

Customers (Debtors)

Your customer relationships are very important and you should manage them effectively. Always listen to what your customer wants and thinks should be improved. The delicate balancing act between giving the customer what they want and providing a profitable product is important to achieve. A successful company should know where that balance is and how to achieve it, through a constant flow of information from your customer base through to your product development function.

A good customer may recommend you to others and thereby become an extension of your sales and marketing resource. Likewise a bad customer experience could cost you business with other customers, so try to keep in touch with how your customers are feeling about your products and ask for feedback.

Directors

While you are likely to be a statutory director of your company, it is probable that you will have at least one other director, whether or not you choose this individual personally. It may be someone you have chosen because of their business acumen or a complementary characteristic; or perhaps your financier requires a seat on the board as a condition of providing funding. Either way, the directors are responsible collectively for the corporate governance of the company and should be able to represent the business in its best possible light.

Make sure you are aware of the capabilities and other business interests of your directors. It may be that a director has a contact at or relationship with a customer, supplier or other relevant party that could be beneficial to your company. It is also important to balance this with the concept that transactions and decisions made by directors should be made 'at arms length', whereby no preferential or non-market behaviour is carried out.

Government

The government offers many initiatives aimed at helping the small business get started. It is worth contacting your local council as well as national government departments (with the Inland Revenue as your starting point), to learn exactly what is on offer for entrepreneurs hoping to start a new small business. Government officials can be both a great ally and a hindrance to your enterprise as they can offer extremely helpful advice and even financial assistance, and yet their objectives are politically motivated so they will rarely be flexible with regard to your specific business requirements. Never be afraid to ask for help from local government departments, such as your borough council, who often run small business initiatives. Business Link is a particularly valuable source of advice and business networking. There are separate branches operating in each county.

Neighbours, local business community

You may be surprised at how many other small businesses are operating locally. These can be tucked away in business parks, in home offices, or as members of local networks. Take the time to find out about businesses that are close to you as there are many advantages in meeting like-minded individuals and other start-up businesses. Again, refer to your local council for advice, and read the local news for information about meetings and networking events. Look out for the opportunity to share office or storage space; couriers and delivery firms could also be shared. Be open to opportunities cropping up in unlikely places.

Special interest groups

Special interest groups exist to report on and assist those people and companies that operate in particular industries, or who offer specific types of product to the market. Find out, as part of your marketing strategy, whether there are any special interest groups locally that are relevant to your business and product. Often special interest groups might report on a new product that can improve the way their members perform a task. This type of reporting could be highly beneficial in breaking into a niche market that is suitable for your product. Marketing of this type is also generally quite cost-effective and often free.

Suppliers (Creditors)

Your creditors are likely to be companies with a profit motive themselves. They will want timely payment in line with agreed payment terms. You are likely to want to extend terms as much as possible; and so the negotiating begins. Try to establish good terms with your suppliers and make sure you do not upset them too much during this tug-of-war as it could cost you in terms of rates agreed, or timely delivery of goods. It is always a delicate balance to maintain goodwill while being aggressive on price to ensure you get the most out of this important stakeholder.

Activity: Identify your stakeholders

Make a list of those parties who are likely to become stakeholders in your business. Fill out the table below with the stakeholder type, contact name and the benefits or opportunities that may be derived from the relationship. The table gives one example. Once completed, follow up with these contacts to ensure you make the most of these important external resources.

Stakeholder type	Contact name	Potential opportunity
Shareholder	John Brown	Knowledge of the industry. Contacts in distribution network. Possible discounts?

Conclusion

Stakeholders are a benefit to start-ups and small businesses. Be aware of who your stakeholders are and investigate the full potential of the value of their relationships and operational decisions on your business. Keeping every stakeholder happy all of the time will be impossible, but it is important to find an approach to managing your stakeholder relationships that works for your company.

5

Key points to remember

When planning to hire a team, ask yourself the following questions:

- ▶ Do I have skills that are best performed solo or as part of a team?
- ▶ Am I better off teaming up with someone with complementary skills?
- ▶ Who can I afford?
- ▶ Which areas of business are my strongest and weakest points?
- ▶ What are the market expectations for my skills: am I as marketable as I think I am?
- ▶ What is my maximum capacity?

When considering whether or not to work with your partner or friend, use the following guidelines to help the process:

- ▶ Set clear lines of responsibility.
- ▶ Conduct monthly progress reviews and provide each other with constructive feedback.
- ▶ Communicate.
- ▶ Set clear lines between work and personal life.
- ▶ Respect each other's opinions.

When considering what type of person you require, consider the following:

- ▶ Establish what functions the company needs to fulfil, in order to operate to its full projected ability.

- Identify the gaps in the range of functions.
- Calculate your budget for staff.
- Research similar job advertisements.
- Advertise the position in relevant press or use a recruitment consultant.
- Prepare for the interview with a list of business and personal questions.
- Carry out the interviews in your place of work (if possible).
- Hire the right person based on information from interviews, their experience as per their CV, and your gut feel about the individual as a person.

When considering the way your team functions, make sure you cover the following roles or departments within your company:

- Product development
- Sales
- Marketing
- Operations and logistics
- Administration
- Finance

Consider external resources that are available to all small business, as well as those that are unique to your own. Look around you; these resources may include:

- Banks
- Competitors
- Customers (debtors)
- Directors
- Government
- Neighbours
- Local business community
- Special interest groups
- Suppliers (creditors)

SECTION

6

Framework

You are now at the stage where you need to think about the framework in which to operate your new venture. Many entrepreneurs have questions such as, 'Am I allowed to operate a business from home?', 'Is working from home seen as unprofessional?' and 'What are the legal requirements for a customer contract?' This chapter will answer these questions and address other points that any entrepreneur should know before setting up their business.

Chapter 16 – How can the law help protect your Big Idea and company?

Small business owners should have an awareness of the intellectual property protection options available to them and the differences between them. Often terminology is misused or misunderstood – by both business owners and investors – so learn the difference between patents, copyright, design and trademarks.

Contract law is an essential part of running a business. It often falls to the directors or the owner to take responsibility for this function. It needn't be daunting, provided the basic principles are understood and followed.

Chapter 17 – What framework should you use to sell your product?

Deciding whether to operate as a sole trader or within a limited liability framework needn't be complicated, as one or the other should stand out as the best option for you. But first, you need to be aware of what each business model entails. This chapter compares the two options and provides information on how to decide what is best for your business. This chapter also considers other issues, such as choosing your legal company name and where to locate your business. All these points should be addressed before you complete the start-up of your new business.

CHAPTER SIXTEEN

How can the law help protect your Big Idea and company?

While there are many areas of law that are relevant to business, there are two that are of particular importance to any small business owner. The first of these is patent and copyright law; and the second is contract law. As your business commences and progresses you may require knowledge of additional areas of law, but before you start, make sure you understand these two key areas first.

Patents and copyrights

Intellectual property (IP) protection should be used to safeguard any invention that has been created or product that is in development. Protecting any new idea or product will increase your chances of success by restricting copycat products and increasing the value of your business. Many investors will expect to see your ideas or products protected, with some form of legal safeguard. The next section will help you work out which level of protection is suitable for your idea, product and business venture. There are four main forms of IP that we will look at in turn. These are:

▶ Patents
▶ Copyright
▶ Designs
▶ Trade marks

Patents

The term 'patent' is used by many inventors, business owners and investors. While the term seems sometimes to be used indiscriminately to cover all four categories of IP protection as listed in this chapter, it is important that you understand the distinction between each category.

A patent is a licence that is granted to protect an invention or a new idea. An invention, by its very definition, must be inventive; this aspect will be tested during the patent application process. You must be the legal owner of your invention to apply for a patent, so ensure that it has been developed entirely by yourself and not through any prior employment or in partnership with another party who may wish to claim ownership.

The application for a patent can take up to three years to be finalised. The patent will be granted by the government-run Intellectual Property Office (IP Office), which will be thorough in making sure that your invention is sufficiently unique to warrant a licence, as these can be of great value to an inventor and are highly contested should any dispute over its origins arise. Once you have your unique invention, contact the IP Office to commence your patent application without delay.

Copyright

Copyright exists to protect the interests of those who produce written, dramatic, musical, artistic, audio-visual and electronic works. Copyright is automatic, provided you have created a new idea. Registration of copyright is automatic. It does not need to be registered, although it is suggested that you mark your work with the copyright symbol ©. Also include the name of the copyright holder and the year that it was created. While this is not essential, it expresses the individuality of the concept behind your Big Idea.

You are able to sell or transfer your copyright to another party should you wish to do so.

Designs

If your Big Idea is a design or is accompanied by a design, you should register it with the IP Office. You should include any design that is material to the individuality of your Big Idea, such as specifications and technical function as well as marketing designs that you may want to use to brand your product. Designs can be registered for up to 25 years, so make sure you are satisfied with what you wish to register. Remember that the design you create must be new, so ensure that you carry out your competitive research and analysis diligently to ensure that you meet the requirements for registration of a design.

Trademarks

A trademark refers to a sign or symbol and is commonly referred to as a 'badge of origin' as it is used to differentiate a product from its competitors. You must register a trademark with the IP Office. Successful registration will be offered only to trademarks that are sufficiently unique and distinctive.

The following table shows the four different types of protection and how they differ from each other.

	Copyright	Designs	Patents	Trademarks
Transferable	Yes	Yes		
Automatic	Yes	No – must register	No – must apply	No – must apply
Cost	0	£35-£60	£200	£200
Actions required	Mark your work with the © symbol	Register with the IP Office	Apply at IP Office using Form 1/77	Apply at IP Office using Form TM3

Further useful information can be found at the government-run website www.ipo.gov.uk.

Contract law

It is important for any business owner to appreciate the basics of the legal framework within which he or she operates: to understand how the law impacts on decisions that he makes about his business, and how it impacts on other businesses too. Thorough knowledge of contract law at an early stage can save a lot of time, money and anxiety at some future point in the life of the business.

Contracts are essential in business, and they are everywhere. We all make contracts everyday, whether in written or verbal format. A small business owner should understand and be able to navigate a basic business contract to ensure that the business is not exposed to risk unnecessarily. Contracts are no less important in a small start-up than in a large multinational corporation; and are sometimes more so, as small businesses have fewer defences and mistakes can be costly. It is unusual for a small business to be able to afford to recruit a dedicated legal advisor, so this role normally falls to the owner. However, it is not difficult to grasp the basics of contract law. Once the basic terminology has been learned, contract negotiation will become second nature and handling your own negotiations may save the company both financially and in terms of reputation. (Note that this chapter draws upon the concepts of UK contract law only.)

What is a contract?

A contract is an exchange of promises between parties that is considered legally binding. Sometimes a contract must be in writing to be legally binding, but more often a verbal contract is sufficient. It is important to know how a contract is constructed, as well as what format it must take to be legally binding. There are three elements to the formation of a contract:

1. Offer and acceptance

2. Consideration

3. Intention to create a legal obligation

Let's look at each of these essential elements of a contract in turn.

Offer and acceptance

The most important feature of a contract is offer and acceptance, which requires one party to make an offer for a specific transaction, which is then accepted by another party. A contract will be formed when each party can provide evidence that they will conduct the transaction with the intention of fulfilling their obligations, as defined by a reasonable person. Offer and acceptance does not always need to be expressed orally or in writing. A contract may also be implied and therefore not be required to be in writing or to be signed.

If you phone a painter and ask for him to visit your office to paint a new sign outside your building, you are entering into a contract. He comes to the office and performs the job as required. You are required by law to pay the painter his fee for the work as it was 'implied' that you would do so when you asked him to do the work. If you do not pay the painter his fee, you are in breach of contract despite no paper having been signed.

Consideration

The concept of consideration is that each party must provide to the other contractual parties something of perceived value. This can be an area of contention as the perception of value can differ between parties and therefore it is very important that any issues of consideration, namely payment, be agreed and carefully recorded in sufficient detail as part of the body of the contract. This is a common area for mistakes and ambiguity. If in doubt, include more detail rather than less to avoid misinterpretation of the consideration due to each party. There are three rules that control consideration, these are:

1. Consideration must be sufficient, but need not be adequate. A contract to purchase office equipment can be satisfied with the amount of £1 stated as consideration, provided that each party has read and understands the contractual obligation.

2. Consideration must be present or future value and therefore must not be from the past. For example, when entering into a contract to supply goods to a customer, past payment or credits cannot be carried forward into the contract.

3. Consideration must move from the party who is making the promise of payment. If there are several parties to the contract, the rule is that the consideration must move from the party who is making the promise – it needn't travel to the party to whom the goods or services are being delivered.

Intention to create a legal obligation

There is an assumption in contract law that if parties enter into a contract, their intention is to create a legal obligation. This is easily argued in terms of a business meeting with negotiations surrounding an existing or future transaction, however if there is a situation whereby there is no intention to enter into a legally binding contract, this should be clearly stated. Without stating an intent to remain free from legal obligation, you may become a party to a contract to which you do not wish to be bound. As with all areas of contract law, make your true intentions known to all relevant parties.

Format

We've all heard the saying, 'it's not worth the paper it's written on', but how do we know if a contract is actually a contract and when does a contract have to be in writing? As we saw in the section on offer and acceptance, a contract needn't be in writing for it to be legally binding. There are, however, some contracts that must be in writing to allow parties to use the law as remedial action should another party not fulfil an obligation.

Guarantees and the sale and purchase of land are among the types of contracts that must be in writing. The law does not require many business contracts to be in writing; however, it makes good business sense to enter into a formal written contract for all material agreements to which the company is a party. The company should reduce its exposure to risk wherever possible, through the use of contracts.

Written contracts that may be entered into should include:

▶ Employment contracts – detailing full remuneration package and entitlements along with any regulations on company policy.

▶ Freelance labour contracts – including details of rates per day and hour.

▶ Leases – such as building, office equipment, and motor vehicle.

▶ Customer and supplier contracts – which should note all issues specific to those parties; such as payment terms, product specification, minimum orders and delivery agreements.

▶ Shareholder agreements – detailing the number of shares and associated consideration.

In the context of running a small business, it would be impractical and it is not essential to enter into a contract with each of the stakeholders in your business. For example, you do not need to sign a contract when you purchase stationery; however if you buy items on credit, there will often be a set of terms and conditions included either on a website or the back of an invoice. Upon order and receipt of these goods you are entering into the terms of the supplier and that is a contract.

Conclusion

You do not need to be a lawyer to make sure you use the law to protect and help your business. Following basic principles to ensure your product is protected can be a significant selling point for your business. Having exclusivity in an idea, concept or design can make your company much more attractive to investors and ultimately potential buyers for your business. Similarly, a basic knowledge of contract law can save you costly mistakes and clarify the expectations and obligations of your business.

17

What framework should you use to sell your product?

Once you have developed your product, done your market research and know who you want working for you, it is time to think about the framework in which you will operate. There are two main routes that you can follow when considering how to conduct your business; these are sole trader and limited company.

Sole trader

Often the simplest way to start trading is to set up as a sole trader. The income of the business and that of the sole trader personally are counted together and treated as one when they are reported and taxed. You will retain control over your business and accounting activities and the only reporting required is your self-assessment tax return at the end of the tax year. There is no further disclosure required. It is still important, however, to retain up-to-date, accurate accounting records of your trading activity.

The main consideration for a sole trader is that there is no protection against adverse trading and any debts that may arise as a result. The sole trader is personally liable for any trading debts and his personal assets may be called upon to settle outstanding amounts. This can lead to the bankruptcy of the sole trader as there is no legal protection from his creditors.

Limited company

Setting up a limited company is relatively straightforward and is the most common framework under which companies operate in the UK . The reason it is called a limited company is that the liability of the directors is limited and therefore there is a certain amount of protection against adverse trading activity resulting in debts.

A limited company can be incorporated through Companies House using four simple documents:

▶ Memorandum of association

▶ Articles of association

▶ Form 10

▶ Form 12.

The first two forms are available from legal stationers for a small fee; forms 10 and 12 are available free from Companies House. There is generally no need to use a solicitor or accountant to aid in incorporating a limited company.

As a director of a limited company, there are fiduciary duties that must be upheld with regards to the shareholders (that is, there is a legal responsibility to act in shareholders' interests). The trading activities of a limited company can be scrutinised in more detail than those of a sole trader, therefore all decisions taken must be in the best interests of all concerned. The duty of directors also extends to stakeholders, such as creditors, debtors and employees; so the actions of the statutory directors must be seen to be meeting the requirements of all of these parties, where possible.

However, many other commercial aspects of running a limited company, such as accounting, actual operations, VAT and insurance, are the same as operating as a sole trader, as listed in the table following:

	Sole trader	Limited company
Set up	Simple, register with Inland Revenue.	Incorporate company with Companies House.
Owner/director liability	Unlimited – personally liable for trading debts.	Limited liability for directors.
Reporting	Year end self-assessment tax return.	Year end statutory accounts, annual return, corporation tax return.
Tax	Personal income thresholds apply.	Corporation tax rates apply.
VAT	Not automatic, register when income exceeds £64,000 (2007/08).	Not automatic, register when turnover exceeds £64,000 (2007/08).
Insurance	Public liability, employer's liability and other relevant trade insurance recommended.	Public liability, employer's liability and other relevant trade insurance recommended.
Bank account	Account in private name sufficient.	Separate company bank account required.

Generally, it is more popular to incorporate a limited company for any significant trading activity in the UK. The overriding reason for this is the protection of limited liability offered to directors, and the professional image conveyed by the framework of a limited company. While reporting for a limited company is undoubtedly more complicated and detailed, it needn't be a burden provided all records are kept up-to-date and the directors conduct themselves in a professional manner.

Choosing your company name

In chapter seven, we covered the commercial aspects of choosing a name for your product or trading company. In this section, we look at your legal company name. Your legal company name can be different from the name under which you trade, such as 'A Ltd, trading as B', but generally it is easier and clearer to have the same name for both purposes. You cannot choose any name you wish for your legal company name. There are certain legal requirements concerning choosing a company name and these are regulated by Companies House. As we saw above in the limited company section, you will need to submit incorporation documents to Companies House when setting up your company. It is at this point that your chosen name will either be accepted or rejected. Some possible reasons for a name to be rejected are as follows:

- ▶ The name is the same as (or too similar to) a name already in existence (known as passing off).
- ▶ It hints at a royal connection, such as the use of the name Queen or Prince.
- ▶ It suggests a connection to the Government.
- ▶ The name is considered offensive.
- ▶ The name suggests a banking activity.
- ▶ It suggests a particular status or 'pre-eminence', such as British, England, European, International or National.
- ▶ Its use would be considered a criminal offence.

To be sure about the viability of your chosen name, it is worth contacting Companies House before submitting the forms, to ensure that your name is considered appropriate and likely to be accepted upon submission of your incorporation documents.

Work from home or an office?

Many people who set up their own businesses do so to improve their quality of life. For many of us, that means reducing or cutting out the commute into an office. While a home office can be a cost effective way for a small business to get started, there are a number of factors that the small business owner should consider when making this decision. The following table summarises the advantages and disadvantages of working from home.

Advantages	Disadvantages
Cheap – no additional leases, services charges, repairs or utilities bills.	Lacks the professionalism of an office located in a business environment.
No commute – time saving and less stress.	Meetings can be difficult to arrange if you do not have the space and facilities, such as video-conferencing.
Convenient	Motivation can be lacking for yourself or your team.
Flexible around working hours.	More difficult to hire quality staff.
Comfortable	Clients may be less willing to travel to a home environment for a meeting, so you may need to carry out meetings in a public place or hired meeting room.
	May lack business facilities commonly found in a professional office environment.

If you do decide to set up an office at home, remember the following points:

▶ Take out the right level of insurance on your home office, which should at least include contents and public liability insurance. Seek advice from a broker or insurer before setting up your office space.

▶ You can charge a certain percentage of your domestic bills to your income as a taxable expense, so make sure you keep all of your relevant receipts.

▶ Make an effort to separate work life and personal life. This may mean a lock on the door to deter the kids from walking in on a business call or a sign on the door letting others know that you are busy.

▶ Perception is important, so do what you can to make your business look bigger and more professional. Items such as corporate stationery or the use of a post office box rather than an obviously domestic address will convey a message of professionalism.

▶ Work efficiently as though you were in a large office with its deadlines and timescales. Just because you are working from home doesn't mean you can start watching daytime TV.

Working from home can be seen as a luxury and viewed with envy by those who commute for hours into the office. While there are positives in this situation, you need to be aware of the disadvantages. Make sure a home office and its environment is right for you and the company that you hope to build.

Conclusion

Consider your needs and the projected operations of your company and decide whether the use of a sole trader or limited company framework is more appropriate. While being a sole trader is easier to account and report for, the protection offered to the directors of a limited company should not be overlooked by an entrepreneur starting up a new business.

Once you have chosen your framework, choose your company name carefully, avoiding the constraints placed on this process by Companies House. The next decision concerns where to operate from – office or home. With this level of framework in place, you are now ready to start your own business. The following section takes a detailed look at your first six months in business.

6

Key points to remember

Protect your Big Idea and your company through the use of a legal framework that can be tailored easily to your specific business. Small business owners should understand the intellectual property protection options available, and contract law basics, before starting up.

There are four main forms of Intellectual Property protection, these are:

► Patents

► Copyright

► Design

► Trade marks

A commercial contract should contain three elements in order to form the contract:

► Offer and acceptance

► Consideration

► Intention to create a legal obligation

Decide whether being a sole trader or owning a limited company is the better legal framework for your trading operation. The benefit of a limited company over being a sole trader is the protection offered to directors through the limited liability framework.

► Register as a sole trader through the Inland Revenue.

► Incorporate a limited company through Companies House.

Choose your company name carefully and check with Companies House that it is suitable before submitting your incorporation documents. Some possible reasons for a name to be rejected are as follows:

▶ The name is the same as (or too similar to) a name already in existence (known as passing off).

▶ It hints at a royal connection, such as the use of the name Queen or Prince.

▶ It suggests a connection to the government.

▶ The name is considered offensive.

▶ The name suggests a banking activity.

▶ It suggests a particular status or 'pre-eminence', such as British, England, European, International or National.

▶ Its use would be considered a criminal offence.

Decide whether to set up your operations at home or in a separate office. Carefully consider the advantages and disadvantages of each option to make the right decision for you.

In the Job

Once all of the financial planning, strategy, product development, marketing and resource planning have taken place, it will be time to actually start trading. Your time in the job will be made much simpler if your planning has been as concise and meticulous as possible. Work through the first six sections of the book before deciding what you should do during your first six months in the job, as you need a solid foundation on which to build if you hope to be a successful entrepreneur.

Chapter 18 – What should you do in the first six months?

This chapter considers the requirements of the job from the first day of operational trading of your new business. It includes guidance on what you should review at the end of your first six months and, looking forward, what you should plan for beyond this initial milestone. From the first day your Big Idea is sold to paying customers, you should try to make the process as smooth as possible.

18

What should you do in the first six months?

Before you know it, it will be the first day of trading with your new company. You have spent time developing your Big Idea into a product that you are now ready to sell. By this stage you should have carried out a lot of market research and spent considerable time planning your strategy, identifying your personal goals and attributes, as well as outlining your plans for the business. It is advisable to have worked your way through the key sections of this book before starting to trade to make sure you are as well prepared as possible.

So, here you are. You are ready to start your new job. What should you have ready on day one? Where should you be hoping to be by the end of the first six months? What should you consider beyond the first six months? This chapter will address these three key moments in the early stage of your company's life.

Day one

When you open the doors on the first day of business, or take that first phone call, you should have certain key aspects of your business ready. Your level of preparedness will convey an image of professionalism to customers, suppliers and other interested parties as well as help you focus on the core of the business. Use the following key business areas as a guide to remind you of what you need to have in place:

- ▶ Administration
- ▶ Marketing
- ▶ Legal
- ▶ Human resources
- ▶ Operations
- ▶ Financial

This list should look familiar as it was included in section 5. Let's look at each section in turn to understand the requirements for day one of trading.

Administration

Corporate stationery featuring your name, address and contact details should be prepared and ready for use. Your company number and registered address should also be included if you are trading as a limited company. Your stationery should include an eye-catching logo and be used for all correspondence relating to any activity of the company. Letterhead can be generated yourself and printed on good quality paper to minimise the expense. A little effort goes a long way to convey a professional image.

Make sure people can contact you. Have your phone lines, fax and answering machine set up and ready. Access to information should be effortless. You should have a computer with Internet access loaded with any software that you require. If you have more than one computer, try to have them networked to make life much easier.

Marketing

Marketing information on day one should include the following:

- ▶ A price list for all products.
- ▶ A customer contact list.
- ▶ A plan of how to contact customers.
- ▶ A mechanism for collecting customer feedback.

▶ A plan of where the product is to be sold to maximise sales.

▶ Full working knowledge of the product specification.

Many new businesses plan a launch party or event early on in their business life. However, experience has shown that a trade launch is generally more effective if you wait until the product has traded on the market for some months first. While PR executives and marketers may disagree, there are many other, more pressing priorities to focus on during those first months than a launch, which can take resources and attention away from getting essential operations working and into place in order to receive and deliver orders. Wait until you have reached a level of comfort with the way your business is operating before presenting it to the trade and customers through any official PR activity.

Legal

The main legal consideration on day one is to make sure the necessary contracts are in place. These will include contracts given to you by suppliers of goods and services, which you should have reviewed carefully before signing and kept a copy on file. Employment contracts should also be given to any employee that you have hired at this early stage.

You should also make sure that your customers understand your terms and conditions of business. It is common practice to print your standard terms and conditions on the back of an invoice or order form, or to state them clearly on your till receipt.

Human resources

If you need the help of other people on day one, make sure you have secured their employment before day one. It is generally better to ask them to start work a couple of days in advance to ensure they are trained appropriately, though keep this timeframe to a minimum as you will need to start paying them from the date they start. Define your strategy of employment for the next six months.

Decide what other employees are required (if any) and where you will find them. In a small company, it is often a good idea to make the hiring process an inclusive one by asking your existing staff to participate in some way, for example, by helping to sort through CVs.

Operations

Make sure you can fulfil a customer order. By the time you have opened your doors, you should have practised how your operations will function and who will be responsible for certain tasks. Test the process of taking an order through the following steps:

▶ Process the order

▶ Check the quality of goods

▶ Check the order matches the goods being sent

▶ Confirm customer payment

▶ Deliver goods in promised timeframe

Bear in mind that no amount of practice will prepare you for every eventuality that will arise from actual trading. The process is likely to become more streamlined as you become more practiced. Just make sure that on day one, when the phone rings or someone walks through the door, you can take order details efficiently and provide the customer with the information they want and need with minimal fuss.

Financial

Your cashflow statement should be set up as a separate file that you can update on a daily basis. The balance should tie back in to the actual balance as per your bank statement and it should plan ahead for your weekly cash inflows and outflows. Use the cashflow format used in chapter 11 and simply replace the monthly data with weekly data, so that each week you have every payment and every customer receipt planned for. While this may seem an excessive level of detail, it is important to understand the cashflow of your business.

You can begin to summarise data and make assumptions about cashflow after the first six months, but for now keep your workings as detailed as possible. Monitoring this workbook should be one of your main priorities during the first six months.

Set up an accounting system to account for sales and purchase invoices and any other accounting information. Monthly accounting should be adequate at this stage as profitability will be difficult to measure until you have been trading for at least two months and have the associated documents. In the short term, make sure you keep every scrap of paper and receipt as they may have relevance for your accounts. Once you have started trading, it is important that each of these areas is carefully monitored to make sure you stay on track to meet your goals and objectives. By the end of your first six months you will be able to analyse the performance of your business.

The first six months

The first six months of running any business involves a very steep learning curve. Even if you know your product and you thought you knew your market, you will have undoubtedly learned something new about almost every aspect of business during this time. The key is to identify and learn from these lessons.

The end of the first six months of trading is an ideal time to step back and take stock of your trading history, by carrying out a review of your business operations. Again, use the main business categories (listed below) as a guide and compare the outcome at this stage with your starting point six months ago.

Administration	▶ Are customers and other parties able to contact you effectively? ▶ Are your business premises working to support your operational activities efficiently?
Marketing	▶ What is the customer feedback on your product and its delivery to market? ▶ Are you tracking this feedback sufficiently? ▶ Is it now time for PR activity or an official launch? It may still be early for this activity, though companies generally plan some form of marketing activity over and above the norm during the first year of trading.
Legal	▶ Are your terms and conditions working to ensure customers know their rights and obligations? ▶ Do you feel that you are adequately protected in terms of insurance? ▶ Are suppliers' agreements being upheld? Check through the original contracts to make sure suppliers are meeting their responsibilities as originally agreed.
Human resources	▶ How do you rate your staff in terms of efficiency and appropriate skills for their task? Conduct a review of their performance – address any issues and praise any achievements. ▶ Identify and plan for any gaps in resource requirements. ▶ Ensure staff are motivated, to ensure you maximise their potential for your company.
Operations	▶ Have you identified any bottlenecks in your operations? If so, address these to free up the flow of business from customer order to delivery of your product. (A bottleneck is an activity in the operational process that constrains and limits flow of activity.)
Financial	▶ Are you controlling your cash well enough? Measure your planned cashflow forecast against the amount of cash received from customers; as well as cash paid to suppliers for each main item of expenditure, such as cost of sales, rent, salaries etc. ▶ How well have your performed against budget? ▶ What are the main variances, both adverse and positive in your financial performance? ▶ Reforecast your financial planning for the next six months of the year and adjust your forecasts for years two and three if necessary. Any new information should be included and your financial planning should reflect any change: both positive, such as a cost saving; and adverse, such as a reduction in planned sales quantity. ▶ Start summarising your cashflow as you should now understand the flow of cash in your business. You may want to move from tracking your cash on a weekly basis to a monthly basis. However, it is still important to keep it under control.

Continue to use this framework for future reviews of your business operation. The detail under each category will be different for every company, but you will soon work out the factors that are important to you and your business.

Activity: Learning from experience

Think back over your first six months of trading. Describe one event or circumstance that has happened during this period that you would like to have changed. Once you have described the event, express whether you feel that it occurred because of poor planning or unavoidable circumstances. How would you do things differently next time?

Ask every member of your team to carry out the same activity and analyse the results. Try to incorporate this feedback into future operations to streamline your business activities.

Beyond the first six months

After the buzz, excitement and likely drama of the first six months, it is important to learn from mistakes made and successes achieved. You and your employees will have settled into your roles during this period and will have started to develop the culture of the company. At this stage, make a conscious effort to remember to maintain your personal motivation and that of your staff. Keep the big picture in sight while making time to address the details. It can be difficult to balance the two, but they need your focus and are of equal importance to a small business owner.

The following table uses the key business areas as seen in the first two sections of this chapter to create an overview for the focus of your company beyond the first six months.

Administration	▶ Streamline any internal processes that are taking up too much management time or time away from the core business.
Marketing	▶ Maintain and increase customer interest and demand in the product by further promoting brand awareness. ▶ Commence any relevant and cost-effective PR and marketing activity outside the normal processes.
Legal	▶ Address any legal issues that arose from the six-month review. ▶ Can your terms for purchasing or selling be improved now that trading has commenced? ▶ Check the progress of any outstanding patent or other IP applications.
Human resources	▶ Address any personnel issues that have been identified. It might be time to reallocate tasks or even replace problematic staff. ▶ Remember to continue to motivate your staff. Now that the initial buzz is starting to wane, your team might need extra incentives or motivation to carry on working to their full potential.
Operations	▶ Stick to the core business. It's too soon to branch into any activity that is not core, as this is likely to dilute your attention and the resources of your business. ▶ If order delivery can be improved upon, put a new or revised operations plan in place. ▶ Fix any bottlenecks in the operational process that were identified in the six-month review.
Financial	▶ Monitor cashflow on a weekly basis – this can now be in a more summarised format. ▶ Calculate and monitor the efficient use and level of working capital required. ▶ Start building your detailed financial plan for next year.

This checklist will work for you throughout the life of your company, so try to build a six-monthly or even quarterly review of these key business areas into normal business practice going forward.

Conclusion

The first six months of business is an exciting time. It is also a very steep learning curve for most entrepreneurs – even those who have proven experience in a business environment. Each business will provide different challenges and methods of best practice. The key to success is to embrace these challenges and overcome them with adequate planning, good management and organisation. Keep monitoring your business through the key areas given in this chapter and stay ahead of any issues that may arise when you start up your own business.

7

Key points to remember

Use the following key areas of your business to plan effectively for day one in the job:

- ▶ Administration
- ▶ Marketing
- ▶ Legal
- ▶ Human resources
- ▶ Operations
- ▶ Financial

Day one should be about getting the essentials right, such as making sure you can be contacted and that customer orders are successfully fulfilled. Everything else can build from there.

Conduct a full review of operations at the end of your first six months in the job. Use the six categories above as a framework. Include everyone in your company in the review and ask the opinions of your staff and for input from those close to the business.

From the six months point onwards, continue to appraise your business activities using the framework and remember to keep your motivation and that of your team high.

Bibliography

BPP Publishing (2002) *Management Accounting – Business Strategy,* London: BPP Publishing.

Maitland, I. (1996) *Successful Business Plans,* London: Hodder and Stoughton.

Saunders, M., Lewis, P. and Thornhill, A. (2003) *Research Methods for Business Students,* Essex: Pearson Education.

Silbiger, S. (1993) *The 10 Day MBA,* New York: William Morrow and Company.

Index